KEEP ON FIGHTING

KEEP ON FIGHTING

The Life and Civil Rights Legacy of Marian A. Spencer

Dorothy H. Christenson

Introduction by Mary E. Frederickson

OHIO UNIVERSITY PRESS

Athens

Ohio University Press, Athens, Ohio 45701
ohioswallow.com

Printed in the United States of America
Ohio University Press books are printed on acid-free paper ⊗ ™

24 23 22 21 20 19 18 17 16 15 5 4 3 2 1

The publication of this book was made possible in part by financial
support from the Stephen H. Wilder Foundation.

All photographs courtesy of Marian Alexander Spencer unless otherwise noted.
Frontispiece: Marian Spencer at her home during the taping of a video interview for
the Woman's City Club centennial celebration, November 11, 2013.
Photo by Tim Kraus, courtesy of Barbara Wolf

Library of Congress Cataloging-in-Publication Data

Christenson, Dorothy H., 1938–
 Keep on fighting : the life and civil rights legacy of Marian A. Spencer / Dot Christenson ;
introduction by Mary E. Frederickson.
     pages cm
 Includes bibliographical references and index.
 ISBN 978-0-8214-2171-0 (hc : alk. paper)—ISBN 978-0-8214-2194-9 (pb : alk. paper)—
ISBN 978-0-8214-4533-4 (pdf)
 1. Spencer, Marian A. (Marian Alexander), 1920– 2. African American civil rights
workers—Ohio—Cincinnati—Biography. 3. Women civil rights workers—Ohio—
Cincinnati—Biography. 4. Civil rights workers—Ohio—Cincinnati—Biography. 5. African
Americans—Civil rights—Ohio—Cincinnati—History—20th century. 6. Civil rights
movements—Ohio—Cincinnati—History—20th century. 7. Cincinnati (Ohio)—Race
relations. 8. Cincinnati (Ohio)—Biography. I. Title.
 F499.C553S643 2015
 323.092—dc23
 [B]
                                    2015013623

CONTENTS

ILLUSTRATIONS

1955–present

PREFACE

THIS IS the story of an outstanding, lifelong fighter for civil rights who, in her ninety-fifth year, continues to fight for change as an active member of the NAACP, the Urban League, the National Underground Railroad Freedom Center, and other organizations. Marian Alexander Spencer's contributions to racial justice and the civil rights movement place her name alongside the courageous women and men who have committed their lives to insuring human rights and dignity for all American citizens, especially African Americans.

Marian Alexander Spencer's impact has been profound in Cincinnati, in the state of Ohio, and on a national level. She was responsible for the desegregation of Cincinnati's Coney Island amusement park and YWCA summer camps and pools nationally in the early 1950s, more than a decade before there was a national civil rights movement. She and her twin sister, Mildred, were the first African Americans inducted into the National Honor Society as high school juniors in 1936. Marian was the first black female to run for the Cincinnati Public School Board in 1973 in a city that ignored desegregation mandates well into the 1970s. She was the first African American woman elected to the presidency of the Cincinnati NAACP chapter and to Cincinnati City Council, where she also served as vice mayor. Marian's uniqueness, throughout her long life, has been her ability to work with both the black and white communities to gain equality for all. She brought change to her small town high school in Gallipolis, Ohio; as a student at the University of Cincinnati; then as a parent, elected official, and concerned citizen.

This is Marian's story. She and her husband, Donald A. Spencer, have been an incredible team, working both together and separately for seventy years to face the racial challenges of the twentieth century. This narrative provides an important perspective to Americans today, particularly white Americans who have never coped with, or indeed learned about, years of official and de facto segregation, and to young black people who did not experience formal segregation in America. Most school textbooks and local histories do not include the many discriminatory facts important to our history that are well known to the older African American community.

Marian's story includes four decades of groundwork leading up to the momentous passing of the Civil Rights Act of 1964. The five decades since then have brought significant change in Ohio and elsewhere, in no small part due to the tireless work of Marian and Donald A. Spencer.

Marian's papers from her presidency of the NAACP and her role as a Cincinnati City Council member and vice mayor, and her leadership papers from many organizations, are housed in the archives of the University of Cincinnati and the Ohio Historical Society. There have been numerous newspaper and magazine articles about Marian Spencer and a page or two in at least three local books on African American leadership. Marian has obligingly provided many of her personal photographs to numerous African American, Cincinnati, and Ohio histories. Her personal story, starting in 1920 in Gallipolis, Ohio, has not yet been told. Family photographs in this current collection have not been published previously.

As a longtime friend and colleague working with Marian on Cincinnati local government and fair housing issues, I was among several people who urged Marian to record her stories. Marian agreed to four months of weekly interviews in 2012. The goal was to complete her story as a gift to her family for Christmas that year. *Keep On Fighting* is an expansion of that work. Statements throughout the manuscript that are not documented by notes are from the many interviews and editing sessions with Marian Spencer. Transcripts of the interviews will be added to the Ohio Historical Society and University of Cincinnati archives.

This important civil rights history should not be forgotten. Many of the battles Marian fought remain relevant today. At the same time, many of her lifetime goals to change social attitudes and discriminatory legal statutes have been achieved. Marian has always wanted to be a catalyst to improve and positively change the lives of all Americans. Her life is a great example of how to make change happen. Her stated hope for this project is that her grandsons and others of their generation will know major progress has been made in civil rights during her lifetime, and that she and her husband played a significant role in making these changes happen.

It has been a great privilege and an honor to work with Marian, known and beloved as "Ms. Civil Rights" in Cincinnati.

ACKNOWLEDGMENTS

WRITING THIS book has been an enlightening adventure and a major expansion of my personal awareness of white privilege. In addition to Marian, who spent many hours with me for the weekly interviews, then reviewing and correcting transcripts and drafts, many other people have been very helpful. The most important help has been the support of Gillian Berchowitz, director of Ohio University Press. Gillian outlined what was needed to make this a book of general interest after reading the family version of Marian's story.

I want to thank Mary Frederickson for her interest and support, her strong recommendation that the book be published, and the introduction she wrote without even being asked.

The Linton Writers Group, including Joy Haupt, Lee Meyer, Sue Howard, and Janet Schenk, faithfully listened, corrected, and made clarifications for each chapter in progress. Dr. Fritz Casey-Leininger read large parts of the initial story given to Marian's family and found Vanessa de los Reyes, a University of Cincinnati Ph.D. student, who assisted with compiling the references and bibliography. Brewster Rhoads provided insight about Marian's city council campaign and offered use of his extensive photographic library. Alice Skirtz reminded Marian of stories when Marian was vice mayor. The librarians at Bossard Memorial Library in Gallipolis, Lynn Pauley and Barbara Bernag, were most helpful in locating articles and dates of Gallipolis history. Jane Kay read through fifteen years of Gallipolis School Board minutes and accompanied me there seeking information about the early lawsuit to merge the Gallipolis black and white high schools. Volunteers at the Gallia County Genealogical Society and John Gee Black Historical Center were helpful. Others who read drafts and offered encouragement include the late Susan Boydston, Noelle Masukawa, Mary O'Brien, Cory Osyler, and Dorothy Weil. Last, but far from least, I am grateful to Beth Sullebarger and the Stephen H. Wilder Foundation for a grant to Ohio University Press to subsidize the cost of publication.

There will inevitably be some errors. Marian has carefully corrected several. Any remaining are my responsibility.

INTRODUCTION

MARIAN ALEXANDER SPENCER and her twin sister Mildred came into the world on June 28, 1920, in Gallipolis, Ohio. They surprised both their mother and the attending physician, who had no idea there would be two babies born that day in the family's apartment above Alexander's General and Hardware Store. Ninety-five years later, these two women speak on the telephone each night at 11:30, sharing confidences and news, just as they have since they learned to talk. Marian Spencer was born at a time when African Americans made up less than 3 percent of Ohio's population. Spencer's grandfather, born a slave in Union County, Virginia, had come to Ohio during Reconstruction and made a life for his family as a store owner. His twin granddaughters were born into a loving and stable family during a period of extreme racial violence. One year before their birth, during the "Red Summer" of 1919, race riots in twenty-six cities across the United States marked the virulently hostile climate black Americans faced in the wake of World War I. Between 1919 and 1921, almost two hundred public lynchings of African Americans took place in the United States.[1] Spencer's life was shaped by these events, and also by the fruits of post–World War I prosperity that drew thousands of African Americans out of the rigidly segregated South into Ohio. Nationally, African American culture flourished during the years of Spencer's childhood in the 1920s as a generation of talented writers, artists, and musicians thrived in the creative milieu of the Harlem Renaissance. Less than two months after Spencer's birth, ratification of the nineteenth amendment ended a seventy-year political struggle and granted American women the right to vote.[2]

Keep On Fighting: The Life and Civil Rights Legacy of Marian A. Spencer contains a powerful narrative crafted by Dorothy H. Christenson, based on a series of interviews with Marian Spencer. These two women knew each other as professional colleagues and friends for many years before they set aside the time to record weekly interviews over a four-month period in 2012. Because the original interviews were designed as a gift for Marian's family, what we have here is a life story told in Marian's voice for her children and grandchildren. But because Marian is a public person, her narrative transcends the personal to embrace future generations of the larger American family. This story is important and should be read by a broad audience for three primary reasons. First, Marian Spencer's story combines her personal and public personas in a way that gives us new insight into the development of civic leaders and the shaping of a new political landscape by committed citizens. Second, Marian Spencer's life has encompassed all of the major national and local changes affecting civil rights since 1920. Third, Spencer developed a distinctive style of political engagement, a way of doing politics that has become increasingly rare over the past three decades of growing political polarization. Marian Spencer has much to teach the subsequent generations about resistance, equality, and the meaning of American freedom. We are fortunate to have her story preserved for generations to come.

Marian Spencer grew up believing in the power of democracy to enrich the lives of all citizens, regardless of gender or race. Marian, her sister, and two brothers came of age in the center of a tight family network—a loving mother and father, a devoted grandfather, and a close group of aunts, uncles, and cousins. Wide-ranging conversations at the family dinner table where friends and neighbors were frequent guests and at which "no subject was barred" taught Marian and her siblings the importance of respecting alternative viewpoints, the power of listening to opposing arguments, the value of compromise, and the necessity of patience and perseverance. Taught from the beginning that she was smart, Marian grew up believing that she and her siblings were "capable of doing anything we set our minds to." Her birthright included a strong belief in education, civic leadership, participatory government, and equality of opportunity. These values became the hallmark of Spencer's unique approach to public engagement and, combined with her family's "long tradition of leadership in the face of resistance," provided the strong foundation on which she built her life.

Marian Spencer's story weaves together the private and the public in a way that provides a new understanding of the adage from the 1970s women's movement, "the personal is political."[3] *Keep On Fighting*, like Marian Spencer herself, disarms the reader as we find not a story of unmitigated success and happiness, but rather a nuanced and realistic biography that weaves together the joys and sorrows of a long life. Happiness and sorrow go hand in hand in most of our lives; few escape the cruel realities of illness, death, and disappointment. In Marian Spencer's case we learn how she balanced the good, of which there was a great deal, with challenges that tested her mettle. Marian Alexander's marriage to Donald Spencer in 1940 began a lifelong partnership that brought two strong individuals together. They each became more than the sum of their parts in that marriage. They grew—separately and together. They fed each other's souls and nurtured their individual and collective dreams.

For both of them the personal became political in the deepest sense. Their marriage reflected the equality they both believed in and fought for; their effectiveness as citizens and public servants grew exponentially because they worked together. These two shared a fulfilling personal life, intense love, and a shared commitment to a wide circle of family and friends. At the same time, their partnership had a public dimension and common political goals. When Donald began his real estate business, Marian took the State of Ohio real estate exam so she could help in the office. Years later, when Marian ran for city council, Donald closed his real estate office to work full time on her campaign. This public/private partnership served them both well. As a team they worked hard, enjoyed financial success, and raised two sons. Their political alliance also bore fruit as they played crucial leadership roles in the city and state. Politicians listened to the Spencers; lawyers and university presidents sought their counsel; community activists followed their lead. They constantly used the ballot box and the court to secure democratic change, and they taught others to do the same. Together they weathered the storms of life, including persistent racial discrimination, fear of racial violence, political and legal defeats, and personal family crises.

An active participant in the civil rights movement of the 1960s, Spencer's engagement with civil rights predated the movement and has continued well into the twenty-first century. Her story provides an unusual perspective on civil rights that grew out of her Ohio childhood in the 1920s when she watched the KKK march in front of her grandfather's store; her undergraduate years in Cincinnati, when she lived with a cousin because African American students could not live on campus; her life as a young married woman in a city with no hotels and only one restaurant that would serve African Americans; and her mothering years, when her fight for racial equality included leading the NAACP's three-year fight to sue Coney Island amusement park to stop segregation.[4] Marian Spencer and her husband Donald worked tirelessly to open schools, housing, jobs, summer camps, and clubs to African Americans.[5] An eyewitness to history, Spencer has been on the front lines of the American fight for racial equality since she joined the NAACP as a thirteen-year-old in Gallipolis, Ohio. Marian's professional political work came out of this background, and her career as a politician, social activist, and government official put her on the cutting edge of political and social change for women and African Americans in the United States.

As Marian Spencer's civil rights activism grew into a political career, she took on increasingly public roles in the city of Cincinnati. Historians of women's experience often lament that a woman lived in the wrong era. If only she had been born at a different time, she would have been able to go far. Not so with Marian Spencer, who was born at an optimal historical moment: when opportunities for women and African Americans were increasing; and when more women were going to college, combining motherhood and work outside the home, and seeking public office. Marian Spencer was a path breaker in the 1950s, 1960s, 1970s, and 1980s, but she was also one among many women in Cincinnati and around the nation who were becoming the "firsts"—the first woman judge, the first woman priest, the first woman professor of history, the

the first woman astronaut, the first woman mayor. It was a heady time for women and the list of "firsts" in Marian Spencer's career goes on and on. She was the first African American woman elected to the Cincinnati City Council in 1983; she was the first woman vice mayor in 1984–85; she was the first African American president of the Cincinnati Woman's City Club, and the first woman president of the Cincinnati chapter of the NAACP. As a woman holding public office in those years, Spencer worked incredibly hard as she learned how to secure a political network, run a campaign, and work alongside other members of the city council. Like other women of her generation whose careers grew organically out of years of civic activism, Spencer was more than ready for the challenge.

Keep On Fighting gives us important insight into Marian Spencer's political style, a method that grew out of a rare combination of grace and gumption. No one is more elegant, smart, kind, or polished than Marian Spencer. She has an uncanny way of making political activism look easy and the act of taking a courageous public position seem like all in a day's work. But her unique style often obscures the bravery required to stand up for justice in the ways she has done. A powerful speaker who immediately connects with an audience, for decades Spencer has regularly addressed civic groups, church congregations, and student groups from elementary through graduate school, as well as audiences of politicians, government officials, and academics. She regularly speaks truth to power. Spencer's relentless optimism and positive attitude has disarmed many hostile and determined foes. She has not won every battle she has fought, but she long ago learned to contextualize defeat in a way that prepared her for the next fight. Throughout her life, Spencer has taken the long view, always keeping her focus on the twin goals of equality and justice for all Americans. *Keep On Fighting: The Life and Civil Rights Legacy of Marian A. Spencer* tells us that story.

Mary E. Frederickson
Emory University
August 5, 2014

KEEP ON FIGHTING

I

A Remarkable Family

in Twentieth-Century Gallipolis, Ohio

THE ALEXANDER FAMILY

T HE KITCHEN TABLE at the back of Alexander's General and Hardware Store on Third Avenue in Gallipolis, Ohio, was a neighborhood gathering place for meetings, political discussions, and animated conversation at suppertime. No subject was barred. But one summer night in 1928 was different. Supper was quiet and tense. Marian Alexander and her twin Mildred, age eight, and their older brother, Harry Jr., age thirteen, were told to stay inside after supper. "Mac," Marian's four-year-old brother, was put to bed early, upstairs where the family lived above the store. The girls were told not to run next door to Cousin Alta's house after supper as they often did. This night in Gallipolis all the blacks stayed at home. Marian and Mildred did not yet understand what was happening; they only knew this night was unusual.

The normal, lively supper discussion resumed the next evening. Marian and Mildred wanted to know why the Ku Klux Klan (KKK) had marched by their store. What was the Klan trying to do? Was there a special problem, or was something bad going on, like the murder trial the previous year? The conversation turned to when Grandfather Henry, his brother Uncle Jim, and Mr. John Arnett Mitchell had filed suit to close the all-black Lincoln High School and integrate the all-white Gallia Academy High School.[1] The previous night was the tenth anniversary of their successful lawsuit. They had won.

Marian remembers:

The night the KKK marched was dark, warm, and moonless. There were no streetlights on the unpaved streets north of the railroad tracks where all the Negroes lived. When it got really dark outside, my father called Mildred and me to come outside on the balcony above the front door of the family store. Grandfather Henry and my brother Harry were downstairs with the lights out in the closed store.

The only light came from the KKK's torches that the members held high as they marched right down Third Avenue toward our store and home. They wore white costumes with high cone hats and their faces were covered with white masks. They shouted and I was scared. I wanted to run back inside. My dad said to stay; he wanted us to see what the Klansmen were doing. He felt that if we understood the KKK's purpose was to intimidate us, we would learn not to be afraid. Daddy said they covered their faces because they knew what they were doing was wrong.

All the neighbors had to be on guard when the KKK came because sometimes they would turn on a house and try to burn it down. We always had a shotgun behind every door downstairs in the store and in the kitchen. My dad kept a loaded revolver in his dresser upstairs.

When the marchers got close, my dad pointed to an "anony-mous" man with a limp in the middle of the group. "See that man? That's Jake Livesay who sells you penny candy in his store across the street from your school." The KKK marched on by, but Grandfather Henry and my brother Harry had been on guard downstairs. Sometimes we still bought penny candy after school, but we didn't talk to Mr. Livesay like we did before that march.

Marian Regelia Alexander and her twin sister, Mildred Lavenia, were born in Gallipolis, Ohio, on June 28, 1920, almost fifty years after the arrival of their paternal grandfather, Henry Washington Walker Alex-ander, who came to Gallipolis during Reconstruction after the Civil War. He was born a slave in 1854 on George Washington's birthday, February 22, then emancipated at the age of nine. Shortly thereafter, his older sister, Amanda, took Henry and their two half-brothers, James and Levi Campbell Jr., from their plantation home in Union County, Virginia, to Charleston, West Virginia.

The children's mother, Dinnah, had been allowed to marry a fellow slave, Levi Campbell Sr., after Henry's birth. Both Dinnah and her husband stayed on the plantation after Emancipation. The plantation owner and former master of twenty slaves, John Alexander, gave each of Dinnah Campbell's four children a cache of gold coins to begin their new lives in freedom. Amanda saved the boys' shares until they were old enough to be on their own.

Henry Alexander and Jim Campbell joined the great northern mi-gration of newly freed slaves to live in a state that had always been free.[2] Gallipolis, Ohio, before the Civil War and during Reconstruction, was relatively inviting to African Americans. In addition to freed slaves, Gallipolis had been a favored relocation place for pregnant slaves and mothers with children fathered by their slaveholders.[3]

Gallipolis is located on the Ohio River 156 miles northeast of Cincin-nati. Freeborn African Americans and former slaves settled in Gallipolis on the north side of town, upriver from the original 1790 settlement grounds that comprise a park in midtown Gallipolis today. A spur from the Pittsburgh-to-Cincinnati Baltimore & Southwestern Ohio Railroad, later the B&O, divides the town racially. The population of the town has ranged from just over one thousand residents in the nineteenth century to peak at 8,775 in 1960, then fall to 3,641 in 2010.[4]

Marian's maternal great-grandfather, Robert Sammons, was a prominent Scotsman from Albemarle County, Virginia; her great-grandmother was a Cherokee Indian. Before 1860, the Sammonses had moved north to the village of Guyandotte, Virginia, where there were few slave-holding families. They purchased property and built a family farm and flour mill not far from the confluence of the Guyandotte and Ohio Rivers. The Sammonses' youngest daughter, Regelia, married Angus Carter, a black; the couple became Marian's maternal grandparents. The family stayed on the farm and ran the flour mill in Guyandotte, which became a suburb of Huntington, West Virginia, in 1890.[5]

By 1874, when Henry arrived in Ohio, blacks had begun to find their voice in state and local government in the South and in the border states. Between 1870 and 1876, 633 African Americans were state legislators in eleven Southern states.[6] Arkansas state senator William Henry Grey, the biracial son of Virginia congressman and governor Henry Alexander Wise and his slave Elizabeth Grey, seconded the nomination of Ulysses S. Grant for president as a delegate at the Republican National Convention in 1872.[7]

The rapid ascension of blacks as newly enfranchised citizens raised fear among whites in the South—a fear that spread across the country as former slaves moved north.[8] The Klan, founded in 1866, was determined to continue white supremacy. Federal troops had been sent south to try to enforce the law at the end of the Civil War, but President Rutherford B. Hayes—ironically, an Ohio native—withdrew them in 1877.[9] Southern states immediately enacted Jim Crow laws and practices to limit black rights. African American voter registration was severely restricted or eliminated. Jobs advertised in white-owned newspapers were available only to whites. African Americans, who had held every position in the national railroad system, except that of engineer, from

1880 to 1912, lost those jobs.[10] In the 1890s, as Jim Crow laws became entrenched and racially discriminatory practices spread to become prevalent throughout the country, the KKK's membership declined.

Then, in 1915, the Klan was revived on the West Coast.[11] Their new targets of hatred included immigrants, particularly Chinese workers in the western states; Jews; Catholics; blacks; and members of organized labor. Again, the KKK staged terrorist rallies and torchlit parades, burned crosses and houses owned by Chinese immigrants, and lynched blacks and sympathetic whites. By the 1920s the KKK dominated state legislatures in Indiana, Illinois, Oregon, and Idaho, and held strong influence in Ohio.[12] Documented racial lynchings occurred in Indiana, Ohio, West Virginia, Illinois, and Kentucky in 1920, the year Marian and Mildred were born.[13]

That same year, sundown towns, where blacks could be employed but could not live, were everywhere across the northern and western United States. Signs were posted in hundreds of towns to keep blacks out of town entirely, or to require them to be gone by sunset.[14] The climate of tolerance for minorities and for their involvement in local politics had changed by 1915. Gallipolis was not a sundown town, but, like most towns and cities across the country, it had segregated housing, schools, churches, and restaurants. The town's one movie theater required blacks to sit in the balcony.

Marian witnessed racial fear and hatred:

The year before the KKK marched by our store, when I was about seven, the young man who lived across the street worked as a bellhop at one of the two hotels in Gallipolis. A woman, probably a prostitute, was murdered in the hotel and the bellhop was charged with the murder. He was the only black person close to the crime scene. Jury duty was restricted to white men, and everybody was concerned for the young man's life. Mother attended the trial every day. Every evening at dinner she restated her conviction that the young man was innocent. She had known him since he was a child. He was judged guilty by the all-white jury, as all the neighbors feared, and promptly electrocuted. There were no appeals of a death penalty sentence, at least not for a young, poor Negro in a small town.

They brought the body home in a coffin for his funeral and burial. I was just tall enough to see over the edge of the open coffin. There were burn marks on his forehead and scalp from the electrical cap used for the execution. I knew the death should never have happened, because my mother said the young man was innocent. Ever since then I've always been opposed to the death penalty.

There was another racial incident involving our family when Mildred and I were about twelve years old. One day my brother Harry, who was seventeen, and his buddy Mitchell wanted to cross the Ohio River on the Point Pleasant Bridge to West Virginia, to visit some girls they knew.

Trouble came from a white man crossing the bridge toward Gallipolis. He stopped the boys to ask for assistance in "getting him a clean colored girl." Enraged, Harry and Mitchell beat the man up and threatened to throw him into the Ohio River. Harry didn't want to kill the man, and he stopped Mitchell from doing so. The man was rescued and taken to Holzer Hospital in Gallipolis. He told the police two young men, one black and one white, had beaten him up.

The next morning the police came to our home and arrested Harry. Harry would not identify his friend. Harry was taken across the bridge to the Point Pleasant, West Virginia, jail.[15] Uncle Edward, Mama's brother who lived in Huntington, West Virginia, posted bail for Harry's release. Everybody was worried about what would happen to Harry if he were left in the county jail. A few days later the police took Harry to the hospital so he could be identified by the victim and charged with attempted murder. The white man identified Harry as one of the two assailants, but he refused to press charges. He stated that, except for Harry's intervention, he, the victim, would have died that day. Neither Harry nor any of my family ever revealed the name of Harry's friend because he would have been charged and convicted of attempted murder.

EDUCATION AND VOTING

Marian's grandfather Henry Alexander used his cache of gold coins from his slaveholder father to purchase property and build Alexander's General and Hardware Store. His store was located just above the Ohio River floodplain on what later became Third Avenue, the main street in Gallipolis. The building had a large kitchen at the back and living quarters upstairs. Henry married Lavenia Whiting, a teacher at the black Lincoln Elementary School, built in 1868.[16] Henry and Lavenia had three sons: Roy, Harry, and Claude. The middle son, Harry McDonald Alexander, who became Marian's father, took over management of Alexander's Store after Grandfather Henry had a stroke. Grandfather Henry, though impaired, remained part of the local black leadership. He presided over many discussions at his kitchen table until his death in 1937, when Marian was seventeen.

Grandfather Henry was aware at a very young age that acquiring an education was fundamental to achieving equality for freed slaves. Henry and his sister Amanda had learned to read and write in the Big House on the plantation because they were the master's children. Henry tried to teach his younger brothers as well. Once he was well established in Gallipolis at the end of the nineteenth century, Henry exercised his freedom by expanding educational opportunities for African Americans in Gallipolis.

Most blacks in Gallipolis were homeowners because Grandfather Henry, as president of the Gallipolis Mutual Aid Society, had expanded the 1863 Negro Mutual Aid Society into a Savings and Loan Association to allow blacks to obtain a home mortgage. Area banks refused to lend to former slaves. In 1896, Henry's youngest son (Marian's uncle), Claude Alexander, was denied his petition to enter the all-white Gallia Academy High School.[17] There was no high school for black students. Marian's grandparents, uncles, and others began to strategize how to build an African American high school. When a local property tax levy to expand the all-white Gallia Academy High School was to be put on an upcoming ballot, the black leadership declared they would support the levy only if the building of Lincoln High School, for black students, was included on the ballot. Black votes passed the tax levy.

Dr. Edward Alexander Bouchet was brought to Gallipolis in 1908 to be principal and a teacher at the newly built Lincoln High School.[18] Dr. Bouchet matched the classical curriculum of Gallia Academy and set high standards, including courses in Latin, French, history, and geography.[19] He knew it was unlikely that his students would have access to further education. Dr. Bouchet left Gallipolis to join the faculty of Bishop College in Marshall, Texas, in 1913. But the political debate about the value and importance of a separate black high school continued to be a regular topic of discussion in the kitchen behind Alexander's General and Hardware Store.

John Arnett Mitchell, a former pupil of Dr. Bouchet, returned to Gallipolis in 1915 to join Henry Alexander, James Campbell, and Claude Alexander to file a suit to merge the black and white high schools in Gallipolis. Mr. Mitchell had graduated Phi Beta Kappa from Bowdoin College; his 1912 commencement speech, titled "Race Adjustment," was the first given at Bowdoin by an African American graduate.[20]

Gallia Academy High School enjoyed a better academic reputation and offered sports and music programs that were not available at Lincoln High School. After several years of court appeals, the suit was successful, based on a later school-tax-levy renewal to build a new Gallia Academy High School and to upgrade Lincoln High School. Upgrading Lincoln High School never took place. Finally, the Gallipolis Board of Education was "perpetually enjoined from maintaining a high school of color."[21] The court decision to integrate Gallia Academy High School was extraordinary for its time, coming thirty-five years before the 1954 U.S. Supreme Court upheld *Brown v. Board of Education*.[22]

Marian tells about her family:

Grandfather's other priority after education was voting. Our store was always closed to become a voting place on election days. I would peek downstairs through the stairway banister to watch people vote. If somebody didn't vote, the next time they came into the store, Grandad wanted to know why. We were taught that the ballot box is equal, maybe the only place where color, wealth, or poverty doesn't matter—voting matters. Our store was also where anyone who lived closer to the river below us, on First and Second Avenues, slept on the floor when the Ohio flooded each year.

When my mother, Rosanna Carter, married Daddy, she thought Gallipolis was a very limiting place to raise a family. We lived in Gallipolis because Daddy could not support a family as a musician and Grandfather needed him at our store. Together my parents had four children: Harry Jr.; Mildred and me, usually just called "the twins"; and Vernon, known as "Mac" from his middle name, McDonald. We all lived with Grandfather Henry above the store because Grandmother Lavenia died quite young, before I was born.

Mama was known as the Gallipolis "town psychiatrist" on our side of the tracks. Many women, black and white, came to her to share confidences and seek her advice. Mama never betrayed these confidences, even though she was outspoken on most subjects. She was well liked, and she prized education for her children. She was president of the Paint Creek Baptist Church choir, sewed all our clothes, kept house, gardened, and canned vegetables for the winter. When she was done, she helped sick neighbors and friends. She used to say, "You can't just sit around and snuff ashes." Between my grandfather and parents, they [my family] knew everyone in town. Not much could take place that they didn't know about. Mildred and I gave them a big surprise, however.

Nobody knew Mother was carrying twins. There was not yet a hospital in town, and only one local doctor served the black community, Dr. Rudy Mack. Dr. Mack was a good friend of the family. Dr. Mack was not sure if both of us would survive because I, the first twin, had been cutting off my sister's air supply.

Mildred Lavenia Alexander was given the name chosen in advance, in honor of Grandmother Lavenia, because they did not want her nameless if she did not survive. Dr. Mack suggested that perhaps I might be named for his wife Marian, who was childless. So I was named Marian Regelia for Dr. Mack's wife and my maternal grandmother Regelia. I was born fifteen minutes before Mildred, and we did survive. Ninety-five years later, at least since my husband Donald died, we talk on the phone every night at 11:30.

Mildred was born quite blue from lack of oxygen. My brother, Harry Jr., who was five, ran around town announcing that everybody should come see the two babies: one was blue and one was red. He claimed that the babies cried all the time and they should be called "Alexander's Ragtime Band." We are identical; in baby pictures you can't tell us apart. My Dad called us both "Babe" throughout our childhood in order to avoid incorrectly naming either of us. Only our brothers, Mac and Harry, could always tell us apart.

When Mildred and I were four years old, I had a terrible accident on a breezy spring day. I wanted to surprise Mama by sweeping the kitchen floor and taking out the trash. I climbed on a chair to reach the matches above the stove. When I tried to light the trash on the ground outside, my dress caught fire.

Dr. Mack came in his horse and buggy and put heavy grease all over my burns, most of which were third degree. The burns covered my right arm, back, and right side. The doctor told my parents and Grandfather Henry that I would be alive in the morning if I had not swallowed the flame. Dr. Mack came back the next day to begin the long battle for my recovery. I spent the entire summer recovering in bed.

It was Mildred's job, after my burns healed, to spread carbonated Vaseline on my scar tissue every night at bedtime. Then, for the next three years, Mildred went next door to sleep at Cousin Alta's house so she would not roll against me in bed. I played on the school merry-go-round all the years I was in elementary school, which forced me to stretch my scarred right side and arm to hang on. My dad constantly reminded me to stand straight. By high school graduation my left and right sides were evened out. I learned a lot about patience and perseverance. Everyone said I was a fighter.

Mildred and I were creative children. We spent a lot of time indoors when I was recovering from the burns. We made cardboard dolls and dressed them from cutout magazine pictures. Our dollhouse was made out of cardboard, with a roof that opened so you could reach inside. We made beds and furniture from small boxes and curtains and bedspreads from Mama's sewing scraps.

Mildred and I got to go for an airplane ride with our father one summer day after I recovered. I remember it cost five dollars. The plane flew over the Ohio River Point Pleasant Bridge (the one that later collapsed) so we could see what the town and river looked like from the air. We were young enough for both of us to be on our dad's lap in the small passenger seat. I was sure we were going to slide out the door and plunge into the river when the plane banked right to turn above the bridge.

Another time, when Mildred and I were in third grade, we had our eighth birthday party next door at Cousin Alta's. Alta had purchased two white angora tams for us on a trip to Cleveland. The next spring Mama made white silk Easter dresses to go with our fancy berets. She was pressing the dresses the night before Easter when she accidentally scorched my dress right in the front, just above the waistline. Mama stayed up all night to design and make two silk flowers, one to cover the scorched material on my dress and the second one for Mildred's dress, so our outfits matched. The flowers looked like they were part of the original design.

We learned a lot about life as kids. We were taught we were smart and capable of doing anything we set our minds to. This is true for smart people whether they are black or white. We heard both sides of arguments at our kitchen table, and, mostly, the importance of education and that all people are equal. Everyone deserves respect until they prove otherwise. Grandfather, particularly, was an example of what good leadership could do. My family has a long tradition of leadership in the face of resistance.

SCHOOL DAYS

Every morning my Grandfather Henry woke us up in his booming voice with "Get your education!" Lincoln Elementary School was less than two blocks from home. There were four classrooms, each with two grades. First through fourth grades were on the ground floor, and fifth through eighth grades in two classrooms upstairs. The first bell rang thirty minutes before school began and could be heard from our home. The second bell rang fifteen minutes later. The final bell meant everyone should be seated at his or her desk. Everyone went home for lunch.

Mildred and I loved school and helped each other with our lessons. We were never tardy, nor did we miss a day of school. Once we even vowed to read all the books in the local library when we worked there as teenagers. Grandmother Lavenia had been a teacher at Lincoln Elementary until she died from cancer at age forty. My family knew all the teachers at school.

We followed my brother Harry to the integrated Gallia Academy High School in 1934. There were about four hundred students at the school, including three other Negroes in our class. Harry was a born athlete and smart, but much less interested in academics than we were. He was the star football carrier on the Gallia Academy football team during his junior and senior years. The team won every game and the Southeast Ohio championship for Gallia Academy his junior year.

It was a very big deal when Harry announced at supper that he wanted to drop out of school near the beginning of his senior year. He had not kept up with his accounting postings and he was afraid he would fail the course. My dad was pretty sarcastic and he told Harry to go ahead and quit. If Harry did, Dad said, everyone would know what a fool Harry was. Mama said, absolutely not. She added that young Harry was still under eighteen and that Daddy could be sent to jail if Harry didn't stay in school. The real deciding factor was the next Saturday morning.

I could hardly believe the entire Gallia football team—all white except for Harry, all those very big young men—could fit into our kitchen! They came to plead with Harry to stay in school so he could play on the football team. With Harry's participation, the Gallia Academy High School football team had won every game except one. The loss was because the Point Pleasant team would not play if there were a Negro on the field. Harry had to sit on the sideline. He did make up his accounting course and graduated with his class.

Our whole family was musical. Daddy played the saxophone and had an informal band. Music was an important part of education at our house. Everybody in the family played an instrument. Both my grandmothers played their church organs.

Mama, like Grandmother Lavenia had been, was president of the church choir.

The music faculty at Gallia Academy were graduates of the Ohio State University. Mr. Baylor had band and orchestra and Mrs. Shough was the choir director. They invited all students to join in the music program. I played trumpet, and Mildred the saxophone, like our dad. I particularly liked the marching band uniforms. Mildred also played in the orchestra, and both of us joined the a cappella choir.

Mary Louise Mohr, a white student and the choir pianist, organized a boycott to protest Negroes joining the choir. Miss Shough then required each of the walkouts to apologize to her for participating in the boycott before they could return to sing with the group. One boy never sang with the choir again, even though he marched next to Mildred in the band and sat next to her in the orchestra. Mildred and I did not learn about the required apology, or the boy's refusal to apologize, until after we graduated. Miss Shough did not want us to be intimidated by the customs of the school.

Mildred and I were straight A students and eligible for the National Honor Society during our junior year. Mama went to the school to demand that our names be submitted to the society even though the National Honor Society had no Negro members. She told the school principal she would withdraw us from school and send us to live with relatives out of town if we were not nominated.

Finally, the day came when the Honor Society inductees would be announced, and everyone knew three names would be presented. There was a special school assembly just before lunch. The custom was to announce first-, second-, and third-award winners in alphabetical order. Mary Louise Mohr was announced first. After that, Mildred and I were also brought to the auditorium stage. It was no mistake that Mary Louise had been announced first, but we were so excited to tell our parents that we just ran home for lunch.

Mama was standing at the door waiting to hear the news. She was hiding her hands under her apron. Nobody in the family wanted us to be sent to live with relatives, but Mama meant to carry out her threat if we had not been nominated. The national black weekly paper, the *Pittsburgh Courier,* published our picture and a story headed "Girl Twins Make Remarkable Record in Ohio School."[23] Mildred and I were also co-valedictorians for the Gallia Academy High School Class of 1938.

Part of our education, before we were old enough to get jobs, was to spend several weeks each summer with relatives who lived in bigger cities. Mama felt we should be exposed to larger churches, museums, and experiences unavailable in our small town. She trusted us to be well behaved, and she wanted us to get to know members of the extended family. We visited Grandmother Regelia and Uncle Ed in Huntington, West Virginia, and relatives in Marion, Dayton, and Cincinnati, Ohio.

We spent two summer visits with one of Mama's older brothers, Theopholis Carter, and his wife, Sally, in Dayton, Ohio, when we were young teens. I think Mama was unaware that her brother worked nights at the post office and his wife worked days. We were on our own much of the time during the week. We did household chores, including hoeing the garden and picking potato bugs off the plants. We had time to walk to the library, play tennis on the courts close to the house, and watch the neighborhood boys play basketball and baseball in the park. If some boy was too forward we shared the information and watched out for each other.

Aunt Sally taught us Southern cooking. We learned some shocking stories about when she was a cook for a family in Alabama. When Aunt Sally was upset with how she was being treated, she would spit in the family's food before it was served. It was just like in that movie, *The Help*.[24] I don't think Mama knew Aunt Sally very well, but we learned much from her.

I was sent to be a companion to Grandmother Regelia in Huntington the summer I was sixteen. We talked a lot about when she was growing up in West Virginia. Grannie's family had never been enslaved. Grannie was the youngest child in her family, but she was the tallest and the darkest-skinned. She told me a great story about when she was about seven years old, in 1861, at the beginning of the Civil War.

There had been a battle in Guyandotte, where some of the residents had helped the Confederates capture a Union recruiting station.[25] When the Union Army recaptured the town they were burning down the houses of suspected Border Rangers.[26] Grannie's father, Robert Sammons, the Scotsman, carefully coached Grannie about what to do, and sent her down the hill to the road in front of the farm. Her job was to plead with the Union officer to save the family's property. Grannie stood by the road and waved to the officer on horseback at the head of his troops. Grannie told me what she did:[27]

REGELIA: Good day, Sir.

UNION OFFICER: Where do you live, little girl?

REGELIA: Right there, Sir *(pointing up the hill)*.

OFFICER: Are you sure?

REGELIA: Yes, Sir. My daddy is a free man. He built our
house and the flour mill.

OFFICER: Were you born here?

REGELIA: Yes, Sir. Please don't burn it down. My daddy is a
free man and he works hard to run the flour mill.

Grannie said the officer tipped his hat, told her she should run along home, and he told his troops to move on.[28]

Regelia, my grandmother, married Mr. Angus Carter, a Negro, and they stayed on the farm and ran the mill. They had seven children. Their oldest daughter was my mother, Rosanna. Mama's other siblings included her brothers Angus, Theopholis, Edward, and Jessie, and her sisters, Estella and Regelia. Jessie was a twin, but his [twin] sister died in childbirth. Edward never married, and he lived with Grannie after she was widowed.

I was in Huntington the summer of '36, because the family felt I should keep Grannie company since I didn't have a job in Gallipolis. Uncle Ed was at work all day. Aunt Regelia and her two children, Harold Jr. and Yvonne, lived with Grannie during the school year when Aunt Regelia taught school. In the summers she took the children to visit their father in Asheville, North Carolina. Her husband, Harold Warren, was a dentist, but he had to live at the higher elevation in the mountains because he had developed tuberculosis.

Grannie was over eighty years old that summer but she was quite self-sufficient. Every morning she got up early to fix breakfast for Uncle Ed. She had usually finished the breakfast dishes and was starting to cook supper when I got out of bed. She loved to play the piano and sing. She knew all the gospel songs. She said the best way to remember the Bible stories was to sing them. She could use only her thumb and little finger on her left hand when she played the piano because of her arthritis, but bang away she did. She played the tune with her right hand.

I was old enough to date that summer. A young man in the neighborhood asked to take me to the movies. We got home quite late. The next morning, a Saturday or Sunday because Uncle Ed was home, he asked me what time I had come home. I explained that my date's father worked second shift and, since we had the family car, his father had to be picked up from work at 11:00 p.m. Uncle Ed said the curfew was 10:00 p.m. If I couldn't get home by then, I could not go out. Uncle Ed was kind and generous with the whole family. He had bailed my brother out of jail, he supported Grannie, and he helped his sister, whose husband had TB.

When Mildred and I went to college, Uncle Ed and Uncle Jessie helped pay for our room and board and bought our AKA sorority pins.

After the family's top priorities of education and voting, we all went to church. Sundays were important days. We started Sunday mornings at Paint Creek Baptist Church at 9:00. Mildred and I sang in the children's choir and attended Sunday school. As teenagers, we were at the John Gee African Methodist Episcopal (AME) Church by Sunday noon, where there was an active youth group.[29] Grandmother Lavenia had played the organ there. Once I sang a solo in the AME Church. It was so well received I thought maybe I should become a professional singer in a national choir or with an orchestra.

Sunday evenings we went to the Baptist Young People's Union (BYPU). Mildred and I wrote and usually starred in plays at the church; we had an active social life. The whole family attended the Baptist church for Sunday evening services.

I resisted pressure to join Paint Creek Baptist Church at the annual fall Friday night revival meetings. Mildred and I often attended the revival meetings in our school band uniforms after football games. The congregation was always asked to stand at the revival meetings. Baptized Christians were then told to be seated. Those still standing were invited to go forward to be baptized and join the church. One time, as a joke, my brother Harry told Mildred he was ready to join. When the next revival came, Mildred, expecting Harry to join her, accepted the invitation to go forward. Harry was nowhere in sight. Mildred was baptized and joined the church, but I continued to resist. I didn't think I was such a terrible sinner.

I was ready to take on the world by the time I was ready for college. I had learned the importance of listening to what others thought, planning a strategy when you wanted to change something, and the kind of work needed to bring about equality.

II

Becoming a Citizen Activist

CINCINNATI, ANOTHER WORLD

MARIAN'S MOTHER chose the University of Cincinnati (UC) for the twins' college education because one of their father's cousins, Loretta Manggrum, invited the girls to live with them in Cincinnati while they went to school. Lillian Manggrum, the oldest of the Manggrums' three children, was also starting at the university. Blacks could not live on campus. The Alexanders felt it was safer and less expensive for the girls to live with family. Cincinnati would be very different from Gallipolis.

Many white Cincinnati residents came from the South or had family in the South. Much of the city was sympathetic to segregation, which was practiced throughout the city. Most middle- and upper-class citizens came from different religious backgrounds than the African Americans. They usually avoided conflict by living, attending school, and worshiping within their ethnic group. However, Cincinnati had experienced racial problems fueled by racial tension, employment conditions, discrimination, disproportionate arrests and convictions, and racial profiling since it was founded in 1788, problems that continue today. At least eleven race-based riots occurred between 1796 and 2001.[1]

Automobiles, streetcar trolleys, and the streetcar inclines at the turn of the twentieth century allowed escape from the overcrowded, mixed-race basin near the river. Major industrial complexes, housing developments, and new highways allowed those who could afford to move to do so. This up-and-out migration created the local Vine Street Cultural Divide, which remains a class divide in the twenty-first century.[2]

Vine Street runs north from the Ohio River to the city's northern boundary. During the nineteenth century, wealthy Jewish businessmen and their families, immigrants from southern Germany, lived in elegant homes along Dayton Street in the northern section of the West End, near downtown. When the opportunity came, they moved north, out of the basin to the neighborhood of Avondale. After World War II, these families moved farther out to the suburb of Amberley Village, where there was more space for both Orthodox and Reform Jewish temples.[3] White working-class families, principally Catholic Germans and Italians, moved to the hillsides west of the basin. Protestants and many civic leaders built beautiful estates and homes east of Vine Street, in Mt. Auburn, Clifton, Avondale, Mt. Lookout, and Hyde Park. These upper-class neighborhoods included small pockets of African American homes. The city neighborhood of Madisonville was originally built on the eastern side of town to provide housing for black employees of the nearby large estates in the suburban Village of Indian Hill. Middle-class blacks (predominantly teachers) moved from the basin to parts of the Walnut Hills and Mt. Auburn neighborhoods. Some middle-class blacks also moved to North Avondale, Paddock Hills, Bond Hill, and College Hill.[4]

Most of these neighborhoods are east of Vine Street. With the exception of public housing projects built west of Vine Street, the west side above Mill Creek remained all white throughout the twentieth century. Mt. Adams, the closest neighborhood to the city center, was originally a white, working-class, and largely Catholic neighborhood.[5] Catholic churches and schools were located in every parish throughout the city. The public schools, with the exception of Walnut Hills High School, were dominated by Protestants, poor whites, and blacks by 1970. This east–west divide has been the subject of many articles, editorials, and political cartoons, as well as school-desegregation and historic-preservation lawsuits, with the moniker "Beer, Brats, and Baseball" representing the west side versus the "Wine and Brie Cheese" neighborhoods east of Vine Street.[6]

In 1938, when Marian and Mildred arrived, Cincinnati was still recovering from the disastrous flood of 1937 and the Great Depression. Over eight thousand residents had WPA jobs.[7] But the city's most important political issue, both on and off the University of Cincinnati campus, was debate about the role of the United States in response to Hitler's advances in Europe.[8] Pacifism swept many colleges and universities, causing concern that the students were vowing to take no part in any future war. A University of Cincinnati student poll showed that 1,039 to 35 voted against bearing arms if the United States invaded another country.[9] Those in favor of bearing arms if this country were invaded were 1,060 to 147. One-quarter of the students surveyed indicated they would refuse to bear arms in any war. Opinion about war involvement was split among the entire Cincinnati community.[10]

Despite that division, Cincinnati was sending large amounts of war supplies to Great Britain, due to the city's wide variety of industrial companies, including Procter & Gamble, General Motors, Clopay, and Crosley Radio. Metal foundries and other manufacturers of needed goods, such as machine tools and clothing, also benefited from the war boom. This increased local industrialization and growing availability of jobs drew many new residents, including African Americans.[10]

The black population increased 40 percent between 1940 and 1950, from 55,500 to 75,000. A majority of blacks coming to the city had less education than the white population, their job skills having been acquired from farming and manual labor. Many were ill-equipped for the war-industry jobs that were available. As most were poor, they moved into what became the crowded West End slums. Like other immigrant groups, they populated the section of the city where wealthier residents had once lived.[11]

The Wright Aeronautical company plant, which later became General Electric, was built in suburban Evendale to manufacture aircraft engines just prior to World War II. The first military aircraft engine was produced there in 1941. The plant employed 4,500, including blacks. To allow those African American employees to more easily get to work, some new housing for blacks materialized eight miles north of Cincinnati in the village of Lincoln Heights.[12]

Then, as war grew closer, patriotic citizens stepped up to do their share of war preparations. Cincinnati's Union Terminal teemed with thousands of military men coming and going to war, and local industry continued to ship massive materials to the war effort by railroad and barges. Cincinnati once had fancy iron balconies on buildings throughout downtown, just like those that had been manufactured in the city and shipped downriver to New Orleans. Shillito's Department Store set the example for downtown building owners by melting down their ten-ton marquee for the war effort. Seven thousand Boy Scouts collected metal from hundreds of gas station collection points.[13]

Volunteers staffed a busy United Service Organizations (USO) station at Union Terminal. The Woman's City Club of Cincinnati pressured the USO to include African American volunteer hostesses.[14] The hostesses greeted and entertained incoming military personnel and sent thousands of others off to war nearly twenty-four hours a day. A small group of volunteer musicians regularly gave USO concerts there.[15] Cincinnati gained a reputation as a "good liberty town."[16] But Union Terminal was also the north/south transfer point for black travelers going from the north into the southern states. As trains were segregated south of Cincinnati, all blacks had to move into segregated cars before the trains left town.[17]

THE UNIVERSITY OF CINCINNATI

The University of Cincinnati recognized only one African American organization in 1938—Quadres, its name taken from the Latin, *quattuor principiis*, meaning "four principles." Before Quadres, the all-black University Singers and Players had been the only African American campus organization. In the eight years before the Alexander twins enrolled, the Singers and Players put on several musicals written and directed by Donald Spencer. Then, members of the group decided they wanted to do more than just putting on show productions and singing gospels and Negro spirituals. Donald Spencer and his good friend, Richard Malcolm, reorganized the Singers and Players into Quadres with a mission to: 1) racially integrate every student activity on campus; 2) encourage excellence in scholarship; 3) provide socialization for African American students; and 4) stimulate the cultural interest of African American students by creating a major annual musical production.[18] Early in her freshman year, Marian Alexander joined Quadres, in addition to the Alpha Kappa Alpha sorority and the West End YWCA.

Marian talks about UC:

Mildred and I received several scholarship opportunities at Ohio colleges because of our National Honor Society membership and co-valedictorian status. Mama decided we should attend UC because of our cousin's offer to live with them not too far from the campus.

Mrs. Manggrum wrote Mama that she was concerned about how well Mildred and I would do in college coming from a small town and, perhaps, with an inferior high school education. She told Mama that her daughter, Lillian, had graduated from the prestigious Walnut Hills High School with a 3.2 grade point average and Mildred and I might find it difficult academically at the university. Mildred and I didn't have any problem. I got one poor grade in economics my first quarter because I had never heard of the subject. By the end of the year my class grade was an A. We were separated academically for the first time. Mildred was counseled to enter home economics, but I remembered my high school English teacher who wanted me to go to Columbia University and study English literature, so that became my major.

We learned about a "disagreeable problem" regarding Negroes on campus the year before we arrived there, but it was nothing new to us. It was the same problem our brother Harry had on the football team in Gallipolis. UC was scheduled to play a football game with the University of Kentucky, but Kentucky had a contract clause barring any Negro player. UC President Dr. Raymond Walters tried to negotiate with the Kentucky administrators. The game was played anyway, without any change in the Kentucky contract. UC's one black lineman sat on the bench. But we also learned that President Walters took several positive actions to try to address the "racial problem." He granted a 1934 petition by the colored students requesting their right to attend the Junior Prom and he commended the newly recognized Quadres black student association.[19]

Mildred and I were supposed to help out in the delicatessen in Mr. Manggrum's pharmacy downstairs on the first floor of the building where we lived. The two Manggrum sons and Mrs. Manggrum helped out in the store, also. The plan worked only a short time because Mr. Manggrum thought we were too friendly, or maybe too "country" in the deli. Instead, we got Federal Youth Administration jobs in the university library our first two years on campus.

Mrs. Manggrum was organist at the Union Baptist Church in downtown Cincinnati. Everyone in the household attended church every Sunday. The first Mother's Day I was away from home I thought about how it bothered Mama that I had not joined church. That day I asked Rev. Page to baptize me, and I joined Union Baptist Church.

Alpha Kappa Alpha (AKA) and Delta Sigma Theta were the two African American sororities, and Kappa Alpha Psi and Alpha Sigma Phi were the two black fraternities.[20] All were off-campus. There were about a dozen on-campus white fraternities and sororities. The AKAs and the Deltas wanted Mildred and me to pledge. They were particularly interested in us because of our National Honor Society memberships and our scholastic records as high school co-valedictorians. There was keen competition for each group to have the higher grade point average. We pledged AKA because we were familiar with the sorority from cousins who were already members at other schools. Mildred and I each received $25.00 AKA freshmen scholarships.

The AKA Sigma Omega graduate chapter members mentored the undergraduates, organized social events for us, and, particularly, helped the undergraduates find off-campus housing. Mildred became president of the AKA Omicron undergrad chapter and I was dean of pledges. We met each month, rotating among members' houses. We held dances and fundraisers for scholarships and attended regional conferences. I made a lot of lifelong friends. I also joined the all-black Young Women's Christian Association (YW) downtown in the West End. I credit the YW for teaching me leadership skills that were difficult to acquire in coed organizations, which were usually run by the men.

Mildred and I decided we should move from the Manggrums' home after our freshman year. The Manggrums were already supporting their three children and it was expensive to feed two boarders, despite the small boarding fee paid by our Uncle Ed and Uncle Jessie. We moved to the beautiful home of Mr. and Mrs. Chiles on Melrose Avenue and Beecher Street in Cincinnati's Walnut Hills neighborhood.

I was elected president of Quadres at the beginning of my sophomore year. Miss Melba Bowers was the faculty adviser. She said she could always tell who was black trying to pass as white, so I didn't tell her about a number of light-skinned blacks I knew but never spoke to on campus because they chose to pass as white. Miss Bowers suggested that I should meet Donald Spencer, who cofounded Quadres with his friend Richard Malcolm. Mildred was already dating Richard Malcolm, her future husband, and Donald was living across the street from us on Beecher Street.

We girls knew who Donald was. We often saw him in his spiffy red car when he left home to drive to Douglass Junior High School where he was teaching, or as he came and went for his part-time job at the A&P grocery store. Donald had removed the canvas top of the car, and when it rained he drove with his passenger holding an umbrella. He was a classy dresser and he always tipped his hat to us. We walked forty-five minutes to and from the university every day, and we were never late. Mildred told Richard Malcolm what our adviser, Miss Bowers, said, and Richard brought Donald over to meet me early in my sophomore year.

Donald told me he wanted to marry me on our second date. That Christmas, back in Gallipolis, I told Mama and Grannie Regelia about Donald, how we really agreed on everything important and we both wanted to make big changes in the world.

A LIFETIME PARTNER

Donald Andrew Spencer came into Marian's life late in 1939 and never left. He was born March 15, 1915, the second child of Charles and Josephine Rice Spencer. Donald's father had moved from Augusta, Kentucky, to Covington, Kentucky, in order to attend the closest high school open to blacks in that highly segregated state. Donald's mother, Josephine, left Connersville, Indiana, to live with an aunt and attend high school in Cincinnati. Josephine's parents were a white doctor and his domestic servant.

Josephine finished high school and soon married Donald's father, Charles Spencer. She expected her children to have good manners, show appropriate respect, get a good education, and work hard. She took her children to the opera, symphony, and Broadway shows in downtown Cincinnati, where they had to sit in the "Crow's Nest" (balcony). Cincinnati had many live theaters, singing societies, a symphony, and an opera company before and after World War II.

Donald's family acquired a piano when he was quite young. Donald attempted lessons, but in a short time his piano teacher said she couldn't teach him because he could already play any tune he heard. Donald was an exceptional student. He skipped sixth grade at Hyde Park Elementary School and started at Withrow High School in 1928. He transferred to Walnut Hills High School when his family moved to Walnut Hills from Hyde Park because his dad changed jobs. It cost five cents for bus fare to get to Withrow from the new home and he couldn't afford it.

Donald was writing songs by the time he was in high school. He wanted to participate in the theatrical productions at Walnut Hills, but blacks were not included in extracurricular activities. His response was to organize a youth group at his church where they put on plays that Donald wrote. Donald also liked to swim and he looked forward to using the indoor pool at his new school. Black students, however, were restricted to Friday afternoon swimming classes, after which the pool was drained each week. This practice prevailed into the 1950s.[21]

One of Donald's early racial confrontations was over the Walnut Hills school policy to not allow blacks to attend the high school junior-senior prom. Donald and his friend, Walter Mitchell, wanted to go.[22] They met with the student adviser. According to Donald, the conversation went something like:

> DONALD: Walter and I want to go to the prom.
>
> ADVISER: Oh, you wouldn't enjoy yourselves.
>
> DONALD: We think we would, and we want to go.
>
> ADVISER: None of the other black students has requested to go. I'll have to check.

The boys were allowed to buy prom tickets. They picked "two of the prettiest girls we could find, dressed in formal dress, and we went to the prom." The two couples danced with each other and had a great time. In 1931, Donald graduated from Walnut Hills High School at the top of his class. His grades tied those of the class valedictorian, but that status was denied to African Americans.[23]

After graduation, he stayed in Cincinnati and enrolled at the University of Cincinnati in order to keep his part-time job at the A&P. Donald, the first black employee of that national grocery chain, could not risk finding another job if he left town to go to college in the middle of the Great Depression.

Donald led a delegation to successfully petition UC president Walters to open the 1934 UC Senior Ball to blacks. He graduated from the university in 1935 with a Bachelor of Arts in education and a minor in chemistry. He had planned to teach science and math at the high-school level, but black teachers were not allowed to teach any subject in the Cincinnati public high schools. Therefore, Donald taught social studies and history at Cincinnati Public's Douglass Junior High School. Part-time graduate academic work led to a master's degree in education in 1940. His master's thesis, "Opportunities for Negroes in the Tailoring and Printing Industry," documented that blacks were quite capable at management-level, as well as menial, jobs. Donald's informal adviser for his thesis was attorney Theodore M. Berry, then president of the local NAACP, who became a national figure and a lifelong friend.

MARRIAGE, FAMILY, AND THE YWCA

Marian tells her story:

Donald proposed to me on Easter, 1940. He brought a bouquet of flowers and took me to a Chinese restaurant downtown. It was the only restaurant in Cincinnati that would serve blacks. He said he wanted to talk about our future. I didn't eat anything but had a cup of tea. Donald said I was definitely his kind of girl—not extravagant. I told him I would go home and talk with my parents.

Donald came to Gallipolis so that we could get our license. We learned we had to have my parents' signatures on the marriage license because I was not yet twenty-one. The clerk at the courthouse was a man whom my father had saved from drowning in the Ohio River. He called my dad and told him that one of his twin daughters had been there and had been given a license, and that she couldn't use it because it needed one or the other parent's signature. My mother was in Huntington visiting Grannie, forty miles away. Don and I called her and she said that she would sign our license. Don took it to her in Huntington. Later, she and Grannie brought it back to Gallipolis and Grannie got Daddy to sign it also, so I had both parents' signatures.

My dad did not think marriage was a good idea. What about my education and finishing college? He also worried that if I got married Mildred would want to get married, too. Finally, Grannie handed my dad a pen and told him we were doing the right thing; he should sign. He did, and he mumbled to Mama that she needed to remember she was the first to give me away. I would be just twenty and Donald twenty-five at the time of our planned August wedding after my sophomore year and Donald had completed his master's degree from UC.

That summer and the summer before, I had returned to Gallipolis to earn money for school. Mildred had a summer job in Cincinnati. I went across the tracks to downtown Gallipolis to apply for a waitress job in the ice-cream parlor. My competition for the job was the former Gallia Academy High School choir accompanist, Mary Louise Mohr. Mary Louise got the job because, in 1939, nobody in Gallipolis, or in hundreds of cities or towns, would hire a female Negro to wait tables to serve whites. I washed dishes in the kitchen. Daddy made me stop. My only remaining option was to work as a domestic servant for a Dr. and Mrs. Brown. I earned $7/week, reporting to work at 7:00 a.m. and leaving after dinner cleanup, at 7:00 p.m. My father was furious. He felt it was demeaning.

Rev. Wright married us at the home of my cousin Alta and her husband, Marvin Stewart, in Gallipolis, on August 12, 1940. Our first wedding reception was in the yard next to the house. We got a lot of gifts, but my most prized gift was from Mrs. Brown, who had not been invited to attend the wedding or to the reception. Mrs. Brown asked me to stop by her house for my wedding gift after our Gallipolis reception.

I had never been allowed to enter or leave through the Browns' front door, or even approach the house from the front. I decided that, on my wedding day, I would walk down the sidewalk in front of the house, up the front walk, and through the front door. It made me nervous; it took some courage, but I did it. Mrs. Brown's gift was two small silver salt-and-pepper shakers, but the biggest gift was walking through that front door.

Grannie Regelia and Uncle Ed gave us a second reception in Huntington on our way back to Cincinnati. Donald's parents gave us a third reception in Cincinnati for family and friends here. Donald asked me to buy a proper wedding gown for the Cincinnati party when formal portraits would be taken. The dress I wore for my wedding cost $5.00. It had a gold cloth-covered cardboard belt buckle and I could use it for church and other occasions after the wedding. The new fancy dress, which Donald paid for, cost a good deal more than that.

My brother, Mac, gave me money for my trousseau. Mac always seemed to have extra money. Even when he was a kid he lent money to his friends, always at interest. He was a real entrepreneur. Donald and I got married just before Mac went into the army and was sent to Italy, where he served as an officer.

We got back to Cincinnati a few weeks before my UC classes started. We sublet the apartment of our friends, Hudson and Florida Anderson, for two weeks in Cincinnati's new Laurel Homes public housing project.[24] There were not any hotels or regular restaurants open to blacks. The Andersons moved in with nearby Laurel Homes neighbors to give us privacy. After that, we lived briefly with Donald's parents until our newly built apartment was ready.

Donald's thesis adviser and friend, Theodore M. Berry (Ted), was building a new home at Cinnamon Avenue and Fairfax Street in O'Bryonville. There was always a section of O'Bryonville where blacks could live. There were two downstairs apartments and the Berrys were to live on the entire second floor. There were many construction delays; it was unusual for blacks to build anything new. We moved in even before the Berrys. We had to sweep the plaster dust out as painting was completed. The rent was $42.50 per month, and food expenses were $4.00 per week, according to the records I kept the first two years we were married.

I transferred my membership from Union Baptist Church to Donald's church, Mount Zion United Methodist. Mother Spencer was president of the church choir there. Donald and I were both active in the NAACP, which I had joined when I was thirteen.

The summer between my junior and senior years, 1941, I was chosen by the national Alpha Kappa Alpha president, Laura Lovelace, to work with her in preparation for the national AKA conference. Our task was to propose needed changes to revise and update the AKA constitution. I went by train to Plainfield, New Jersey, to meet with Mrs. Lovelace and the conference planning committee. I had learned shorthand in high school and was given the responsibility of recording and typing the proposed constitutional amendments. In addition to my shorthand, it was a good thing I was a pretty good typist. We had to make several copies of everything on onionskin paper with carbon paper in between each sheet. I used an old manual Royal typewriter. Every mistake had to be erased and corrected on each separate page. I was newly pregnant and had morning sickness. Everybody there was very sympathetic and helpful; they were just glad I could be there to help. While I was there, I met Ethel Hedgeman Lyle, who was a founder of AKA sorority, the oldest black sorority in the country.

Mildred was tapped to be secretary of the national AKA conference held in Philadelphia later in the summer. It was wartime and there were many military personnel in Philadelphia. Mildred surprised all the sorors walking into the conference with three handsome escorts. So many young men were drafted for the war that summer that there were not many available for dates at home in Gallipolis or at the university.

I continued my classes at UC. Late in my pregnancy my teachers gave me a key to the faculty elevator. Donald A. Spencer Jr. was born at Christ Hospital during my Christmas break at the University of Cincinnati, in December 1942. I didn't miss a day of classes. Donald said it was good planning; I said it was just luck.

I had to get a white doctor because the only hospital open to black physicians was the Salvation Army Hospital in Avondale. There was only one maternity bed there. One might as well have given birth at home if two babies were born simultaneously. We had medical insurance for a semiprivate room, but I was given a private room because I was the only black mother in the maternity ward. My doctor, Dr. Artie Matthews, wanted me to go to Christ Hospital because that hospital had better facilities for the baby and me. Dr. Matthews, Donald's good friend who had transcribed much of Donald's music for the University Singers and Players, had lost two wives in childbirth and he told Donald he did not want to put me at risk.

I kept my promise to my father and completed my degree in English literature. Once or twice, when I couldn't get to class because of the baby, Mildred substituted for me and took good notes. Donald and I had agreed that, when we had children, I would be a stay-at-home mom once I finished school. Donald wanted to support the family. I was never at any loss about what to do. I had joined the NAACP when I was thirteen and the YWCA during college. With my friend and landlord Ted Berry's encouragement, I also joined the Charter Committee of Greater Cincinnati.[25]

My first civic leadership role outside college was at the YWCA. After my graduation I became the youngest president ever of the all-black West End YW. There was the all-white downtown YW, and they were planning to move to a new building with a swimming pool. There was no way the black YW could afford one. I initiated several meetings and we negotiated a merger of the two groups. The president of the downtown YW remained president, and I became vice president of the newly merged Metropolitan branch. Part of the negotiations included the swimming pool. The Metropolitan YW desegregated the cafeteria and swimming pool. The YW cafeteria was the only place downtown where integrated groups could meet or eat together.

Still, I did not like it that our YWCA girls' summer camp, in nearby southern Indiana, was segregated. There were different weeks for black and white girls. In 1948, I was an elected delegate to the national YWCA convention in San Francisco. I introduced motions to desegregate all YW swimming pools and summer camps nationally. These motions became national policy at the 1950 Denver conference.

Donald or I attended all NAACP meetings and I worked with the Charter Committee. Charter, as everybody calls it, was well known for major city reforms in the 1920s. Cincinnati was known as "the best governed city in America." The proportional representation (PR) voting system, proposed and actively supported by Charter, resulted in the first black elected to city council, our friend Theodore M. Berry. He became Cincinnati's first African American mayor, and, later, much more, of course.

I learned how to organize a political campaign. We worked hard to increase voter turnout to support Ted Berry's reelection several times, and to preserve the PR voting system. The PR method was challenged in four different election cycles. In 1957, it was finally overturned in a special August primary election, when all the regular voters were off on vacation. The ballot was also worded inversely, so if you wanted to preserve PR you had to vote "No." The defeat seemed very unfair.

Both my husband, Donald, and I had initiated major progress for African Americans when we were at UC. UC was not, however, welcoming blacks in 1950. I wasn't shy about talking about it. The College of Engineering was not open to black students because the famous five-year cooperative education program could not place black student engineers in local industry. The College of Medicine's original charter stated enrollment was for Caucasians only. After I graduated, I joined with the Rev. Maurice McCrackin and others to picket the university. The College Conservatory of Music finally opened its doors to all.

Negroes had not been allowed to live on campus when Don and I were students. When they finally opened the dorms to women, it was one specific dorm with a segregated floor for black women students only. I think by 1950 the swimming pool at Schmidlapp Hall was finally opened to Negroes. Mildred and I couldn't take swimming when we were students; we had to take modern dance. On Friday afternoons the dance teacher would unlock the pool to give black students our only opportunity to swim on campus.

In 1950, eight years after I graduated from UC, I received a call from the office of the UC president. I wondered why he was calling me! I was a community activist and often spoke publicly for the Charter Committee or NAACP.

President Raymond Walters's secretary requested an appointment for me to meet with the president. So I made an appointment to see Dr. Walters the next week. He ushered me to a chair in his office and said he heard I was saying negative things about the university. He was right. I was complaining about the lack of progress in integrating campus programs and recruiting minority students. The number of black students had increased a little bit from when I started at UC in 1938, but not by many.

I told President Walters that the university was making no effort to recruit black students, or to expand opportunities for those already enrolled. He said, "What do you want me to do about it?" I just told him that because leadership on these issues had to come from the top, it was his responsibility. When I saw such leadership, I would include the change in future speeches.

Marian's interest and involvement with UC has never faltered. In 1975, she was appointed by Mayor Ted Berry to the University of Cincinnati Board of Trustees.

Marian speaks of her role as a trustee:

A major controversial change during my board tenure (1975–80) allowed elected student representation on the board. That followed student petitions, demonstrations, and sit-ins. One day, during a trustees meeting, students blocked the small hallway off the main corridor to the trustees boardroom. The chair, Jane Earley, quietly asked me what she should do. I told her to simply tell the students that blocking the hallway was a fire hazard for all of us, and against the law. They would be arrested if they did not allow open access into and out of the room. The students complied. Later we did approve elected student representation on the board. The first student representative elected by the student body was Tyrone Yates, a black student.

Marian remains active in the UC Alumni Association. She and her husband Donald have mentored many black students over the years. Marian continues to receive requests and speaks to UC history and African American studies classes about her experiences. She and Donald are featured in the center of a mural in the lobby of the African

American Cultural and Research Center on campus. Both received Honorary Doctorates of Letters from UC in 2006.

HOMEOWNERSHIP, NEW PART-TIME JOB

From Marian:

We lived in the apartment downstairs in the Berrys' house for four years, from 1940 to 1944. Johnnie Mae Berry was my mentor and a cherished friend. She introduced me to her many friends and every organization I might want to know about. We were both young mothers with husbands who worked many hours. When I became pregnant with our second son, Edward, Donald and I decided it was time to buy our own home. We moved from the Berrys' to our first home on Burdett Avenue in Walnut Hills in 1944. It was a two-family house and, like the Berrys, we used the rent payments to help pay the mortgage.

Purchase of our home was a career turning point for Donald. He knew location was important, but he was surprised to learn how much commission the real estate agent made from the sale and purchase of the house. Donald decided he should change his second job, which was then at the U.S. Post Office. He went to work part-time for Horace Sudduth. Donald said Mr. Sudduth was the best black real estate professional in Cincinnati. Donald was soon a licensed real estate agent. His style was different than Mr. Sudduth's, but within three years, Donald was making as much money working part-time in real estate as full-time as a teacher.

Several other teachers lived on Burdett Avenue. We all called the street "burdened in debt." We were the youngest family on the block and the neighbors looked out for us. After Edward was born, our family expanded to include a dog. Jockimo had been the company mascot for my younger brother Mac's U.S. Army infantry company in Italy during World War II. Mac was decorated for bravery in the war and he earned the right to keep Jockimo. Mac wasn't sure if he was going to live in Cincinnati or Gallipolis after his discharge, so he shipped the dog to us. This mixed retriever was part of the family for the next fourteen years.

Edward learned to walk hanging on to Jockimo's back. When Uncle Mac returned and wanted to take the dog to Gallipolis, Donald said, no, Jockimo belonged here. Jockimo was very protective of the children and a good watchdog. He would growl at me and then run to sit under our grand piano whenever I would scold one of the boys. Eventually Jockimo was diagnosed with cancer of the spleen. We gave him to General Hospital where they were doing some cancer research, and he stayed there until he died. He was used for human research; he was not just an ordinary dog.

My neighbors asked me to take the presidency of the newly formed Cincinnati Links chapter.[26] I was the youngest chapter president nationally in 1950. We raised more money for scholarships than any other Links chapter in the country that year. I was also able to be more active with the Charter Committee, NAACP, and the YWCA after the boys entered school. I made it a point to be at home by the time school was out because I was almost the only nonemployed mother on our block on Burdett Avenue. In order to get home in time, I needed a car. The neighbors were shocked. We were the only family on the block with two cars, but I was home by the time all the kids got back from school. A few times our kids would be sitting on the back steps waiting for me to get home.

Our house was always full of kids. I became the neighborhood counselor, dispute settler, and resource for cookies and snacks. We even became the Avondale Girl Scout Cookie Pantry for a decade. The boys loaded cases of cookies into the basement, and then reloaded them into the Girl Scouts' parents' cars for home delivery.

I was appointed an original member of the Mayor's Friendly Relations Committee after World War II. The committee was established to study the problems connected with the promotion of harmony and tolerance. It was an advisory committee to the mayor. The Mayor's Committee commissioned an examination of the lack of fair employment practices in Cincinnati. I felt this was an excellent report and I lobbied strongly to have the report well publicized. I proposed a speaker's bureau and public meetings to discuss the report. Mr. Bragdon, the chair, told me, "You don't know what we're about at the Mayor's Friendly Relations Committee." I said, "Oh yes I do, but the committee isn't doing it." I resigned. Rev. Venchael Booth was appointed chair after Mr. Bragdon's death. Rev. Booth asked me to return to the committee. I asked him where he stood on proportional representation for city council elections. When I learned that he did not support PR in this leadership position on the Mayor's Committee, I couldn't be part of it. Not long thereafter, city council dissolved the Mayor's Committee and established the separate nonprofit Cincinnati Human Relations Commission.

I was a member of Urban League by 1950. The president lived across the street on Burdett. The Urban League has always gotten a lot of corporate support, and my picketing Graeter's Ice Cream store and the College Conservatory of Music at UC was probably a little too aggressive for them. I think I was not fully integrated into the Urban League early on because I was too radical. After we integrated Coney Island, some people considered me a Communist. I think the Urban League officers didn't want me to be so visible. I always supported the organization, and I understood why I was not part of the leadership for many years. Sixty years later, they gave me one of their first Urban League Glorifying the

Lions and Heritage Awards. I am still active on their executive committee now, and I can say anything I want. I think they are doing a wonderful job.[27]

WOMAN'S CITY CLUB AND FELLOWSHIP HOUSE

The Woman's City Club was the first local white civic organization, other than the Charter Committee, to open its doors to black women. This was so controversial in the early 1950s that the junior division withdrew from the club.[28] I was among the first group of black women to become members. I liked the club's civic involvement and work for positive change. The Woman's City Club has always held civic forums and provided speakers to address pressing issues such as affordable housing, public health, education, environment, and segregation. One speaker, in 1952, changed my life for the next sixteen years.

Marjorie Penny, from Baltimore, spoke to the club about Fellowship Houses that she had established around the country. The philosophy and motto was "Ye may know that all people are equal." That was my family motto when I was growing up. My friends, Rev. Maurice McCrackin and Harriet Rauh, who were white, organized our local Fellowship House. Fellowship House included clergy from black and white Catholic, Protestant, and Jewish congregations seeking to find common ground. I was the third president, after Harriet Rauh. Membership grew to over 1,500 members.

Fellowship House sponsored monthly lunch meetings for local priests, pastors, and rabbis, and had three Action sections: Trios, the Doll Project, and a mixed race Fellowship House Choir. Trios were groups of three—a Caucasian, a Negro, and a Jew— who spoke about all the things we shared in common. They spoke wherever requested: to school classrooms, Parent Teacher Associations and assemblies, church groups of all ages, and community council meetings. There were sixty Trios, including ten made up of honor students at Walnut Hills High School. The group was listed at the public library's speakers' bureau and they were kept busy as racial tensions in the city were high.

The integrated choir performed often and sometimes along with a Trio for a community program. The Doll Project was led by my cousin, Dr. Joyce Stroud. This group made a collection of about two dozen dolls of important people in history including George Washington; Abraham Lincoln; Harriet Beecher Stowe; Madame Curie; Charles Drew; and Sarah Breedlove, later known as Madam C. J. Walker.[29] The Doll Project took the dolls to public and private elementary schools and Sunday schools throughout the Cincinnati area. They talked about the accomplishments of the people represented by the dolls. The children then identified which doll fit the description.[30]

The Herschede family, well known for their large jewelry store downtown, donated their house on Lexington Avenue in Avondale to the Park Board for use by Fellowship House when the family moved to the new suburb of Indian Hill. It was directly across the street from where Donald and I were building our new home. Fellowship House had a resident caretaker family from Hawaii, and a cook who served the clergy lunches and made refreshments for our meetings.

Fellowship House was in full operation when we moved into our new home across the street. From the time Donald and I were dating, we had dreamed of one day building a home overlooking Victory Parkway. Everybody called it "The Boulevard" in the 1940s. Even before the property became available, Donald began planning the house. The plans included space for entertaining, committee meetings, and party space for neighborhood teens who had nowhere else to go. There is a wide terrace outside the floor-to-ceiling windows facing the parkway that we used for many gatherings. The driveway curved away from the street, so it could become a safe basketball court. The double carport could also serve as additional recreation space when it rained.

The house is split-level. The lower level has a Ping-Pong table and room for dancing, as well as Donald's home office and a laundry room. Donald designed built-in cupboards and bookshelves in most rooms and a special lower-height dressing table for me because I'm short. The house received local press coverage, including pictures to show its modern design. It was unusual for Negroes to build a new home in the 1950s. Over five hundred people came by on Sunday afternoons to see the house in the first months after we moved in. We didn't know a lot of them, but we invited them in anyway.

One of the boys' eighteenth birthday parties was pretty exciting. There were about eighty high school kids here. My cousin Joyce came to help me with a small mountain of food to feed the party. The kids were all dancing in the basement. One wall in the dining room has a long built-in cupboard with a hinged shelf that can serve as a buffet counter. The overburdened buffet collapsed. Food went flying in many directions. Joyce and I scrambled to clean it up, including the whipped cream from a dessert that landed upside down on the dining-room carpet. We put the spoiled food in garbage bags, took the bags outside, and the kids never knew what had happened. Fortunately, I had made double of all the food to be served and there was plenty. The whipped cream spot under the dinner table never recovered; the rug was replaced a few years later.

Edward was at home when we had the terrible Avondale race riots in 1967. It [the riot] lasted several days. The center of action was on Reading Road, just at the end of our street. Our street, between Reading and Victory Parkway, was blocked off by the police just below our house. One of our neighbors, a black man, was pulled from his car and beaten. Edward, who is very light-skinned, got home from work and started to walk up the street toward Reading Road to see what was happening. He quickly came back. He said it was too scary and people were getting hurt.

Rioters came the quarter-mile from Reading Road and Rockdale Avenues and firebombed Fellowship House across the street. A newspaper reporter told us that we, too, might be targets during those riots. I ran to take blankets and assist the Fellowship House resident manager and his family as the house burned. I brought them to live with us for several months until Fellowship House was habitable. Later, the house was torn down and the property turned back to the Park Board, which created Stella Park. There's a playground for young children now, but sometimes it also attracts drug dealers.

Fellowship House never recovered from the disaster, probably because the white and Jewish membership were afraid to come to Avondale after the riots. Despite general neighborhood deterioration over the years, riots, and threats, our house has never been vandalized or broken into, or had a rock thrown through that whole wall of living room windows. Several people have said the word in this community is "Hands off the Spencer house."

I have this nice article from the *Cincinnati Post* written by reporter Mary Linn White.[31] It starts out: "What does the president of two women's clubs do for an encore? She gets reelected. That's the first-lady status of Marian (Mrs. Donald) Spencer in both the prestigious Woman's City Club and the service oriented Links, Inc., whose twenty-eight members have pushed projects designed to motivate black youth toward higher goals in the arts, in academic areas, and in career opportunities. Juggling the two gavels may involve a morning call for help from a Uganda girl about scholarship money for studies at the University of Cincinnati and an afternoon appearance at city council . . . Marian's worry now is that 'I won't be young enough long enough to do all the things

I want to do . . . I hope I never feel there's nothing to do. When you feel that way, you die before your time. You see young people like that. We may die of a tired heart, but not a tired mind.'" The article ends about our local Links chapter being recognized as one of the best in the country and it lists all of my memberships, committee chairmanships, and club offices.

Photographs

1905–1954

Twins Marian Regelia and Mildred Lavenia Alexander,
1920

Henry Washington Walker Alexander,
1854–1937

Regelia Sammons Carter,
1855–1941

Marian's parents, Rosanna and Harry Alexander

Grandfather Henry Alexander in Alexander's General and Hardware Store, circa 1905

The former
Alexander's General
and Hardware Store,
1961

Rosanna Carter Alexander,
1887–1970

Mildred, Vernon "Mac," and Marian Alexander, 1924

Harry Sr. with the twins: Marian *(left)*; Mildred *(right)*, about 1929

Gallia Academy High School, graduating class of 1938: Marian (*fourth row from bottom, far right*); Mildred (*second row from bottom, third from left*)

OHIO TWINS HAVE BRAINS AND BEAUTY

The twins' induction into the National Honor Society was covered in the *Pittsburgh Courier*, April 16, 1938

University of Cincinnati freshmen: Mildred, Lillian Manggrum, and Marian, 1938

Mildred and Marian at their University of Cincinnati graduation ceremony, 1942

Newlyweds Donald and Marian on their wedding day, August 12, 1940

Donald and Marian at their Cincinnati wedding reception, August 1940

Marian, age twenty-six, in 1946

Donald Spencer Jr. with his parents and grandparents, Rosanna and Harry Alexander

Marian, Edward, Donald Sr., and Donald Jr. in 1944

Vernon "Mac" McDonald
Alexander, 1944

Marian with the Spencer
family dog Jockimo, 1952

Family portrait: *(left to right)* Donald Jr., Donald Sr., Marian, and Edward, 1950

In 1954 Edward Spencer suffered a broken neck during a school football game. He recovered completely after surgery.

Donald and Marian in Hot Springs, Arkansas, 1954

III

Family Life

NEW CAREER

Donald Spencer was doing well selling real estate part time and teaching full time. He loved teaching, but still was not allowed to teach science and math at the high school level. He might have been considered for a principal position at an elementary or junior high school except, as Marian said, "the Cincinnati Board of Education would never have a principal whose wife might be on a picket line to integrate the UC College Conservatory of Music, the Fourth Street Graeters Ice Cream store or Coney Island." When Donald asked Marian what she thought about his selling real estate full time, she responded that he could sell iceboxes to Eskimos. Donald resigned from the Cincinnati Public Schools after teaching for eighteen years.

Donald A. Spencer & Associates was established in 1953 after Donald was a part-time real estate agent for six years. Donald felt Mr. Sudduth had taught him well. Donald proposed a partnership, which was rejected. Mr. Sudduth might have regretted that later. Daddy's new office for the firm was a house on Reading Road, almost opposite from where Lexington Avenue runs into Reading Road.[1] Our corner of Lexington Avenue and Reading Road has the large Southern Baptist Church on the east side, and Carmel Baptist Church across the street on the same side where Donald's office was. The house was torn down in 2013 for some new apartments. The office was just a long block from home.

The house that was converted to Daddy's office had a covered front porch, with a few stairs down to the front walk that led to the public sidewalk. Mother Spencer gave Donald a picture of a clipper ship at sea, representing the new horizons Donald always sought. It hung in the office reception area, in what had been the living room of the house. When Daddy started his new agency, the boys and I thought that he worked too many hours. The real estate business does not honor normal business hours and days. We all wanted him to spend more time at home, so we made Donald sign a contract that he would always be home for dinner.

Donald founded the Cincinnati Realtists, the black association for licensed real estate professionals who were denied membership in the all-white Board of Realtors. He then went on to integrate the Cincinnati Association of Real Estate Brokers. He was the first African American real estate broker to join them. He frequently told the white brokers and realtors what he thought, even when they did not like what he had to say. He felt the Board of Realtors should have black membership in order to learn the perspective of the black community. Eventually he became the board's president. When Daddy began his real estate business, I took the State of Ohio real estate license exam so I could help in the office when the receptionist went on vacation.

I was substituting for the receptionist one summer when a prospective client came in to see Donald. I explained to the visitor that Donald had not yet returned and asked if I could be of any help. Whoever he was, he was rude and demeaning. He said something about how could I possibly help? He stalked toward the door, so I opened it for him. I was so mad at the man's arrogance and disrespect that I slammed the leaded-glass front door behind him so hard that it shattered. Donald was just coming up the front walk. I was cleaning up the broken glass when both men came back into the office.

I told Donald about the "gentleman's" behavior, and Donald led him into his office. I was seated at the reception desk when they came out. The client approached me, hat in hand, with Donald nearby to hear his apology. I stood up. That man said he had no idea that I was a licensed agent or the owner's wife. He said he would never have spoken to me in that manner had he known. Well, I stretched as tall as I could and bawled him out for speaking to *anyone* like that. That I happened to be the owner's wife was not relevant. After the fellow left, Donald quietly asked me if I really had to break the door to let the fellow know how angry I was.

The real estate office was very successful. It developed, sold, or managed real estate and sold insurance. At its peak, the company owned or managed one thousand apartments with twenty-five employees in the office. When I began my campaign to run for Cincinnati City Council in 1983, Daddy didn't discuss it with me, but he surprised me by permanently closing the office. He said he had worked long enough and made enough money to take care of me, and he wanted to devote full time to my city council campaign, which he did.

FAMILY VALUES AND CELEBRATIONS

Faith in God, family, and community service are Spencer family values. In addition to all of Marian's civic activities and raising two young sons, Mount Zion United Methodist Church has always been an important part of the Spencers' lives. When the Spencer boys attended Sunday school, Marian felt she should help there. She taught the Sunday school youth group for six years, the same group Donald Sr. had started when he was a teen. Beginning in 1952, Donald chaired the church trustees for twenty years. For much of that time he also served as a member of the Finance Commissions of West Ohio and Lexington Conferences of the United Methodist Church. He helped organize the Methodist Commission on Religion and Race, and was its first chair in 1960. Marian said each year when Donald made a family budget the church tithe always topped the list.

Every birthday, anniversary, graduation, and holiday has always been prepared for and has included extended family members and friends. When the children were young, there were six to eight family birthday parties each year. They always celebrated July 4th, Thanksgiving, and Christmas together. Before Marian and Donald built their home on Lexington Avenue, they used to gather at Donald's sister Valerie's or Aunt Mamie's house in Madisonville. There was always music and singing around the piano, cards, and game playing. Later at the new house, dancing, basketball, and Ping-Pong were popular. Marian's mother, Rosanna, came from Gallipolis to be cared for at the Spencers' for the last two years of her life, 1968 to 1970.

From Marian's interviews:

Donald loved parties. My birthday, June 28, was always special. I still like to remind people I was born the year women received the right to vote, in 1920. Our anniversary, August 12, was always a treat, too. For sixty-nine years our wedding anniversary was always a picnic party in one of several parks. After 1955, it was almost always near Fox Lake. One year, we were on a ship in Norway, but Donald made sure there was a picnic basket that included a special small box for me. My gift was always a unique and very special piece of jewelry. In the early years, it was made of copper or with semiprecious stones; as our financial status improved so did the lovely jewelry, often custom-made.

Fox Lake, near Angola, Indiana, where we first rented a cabin for several years, and built our summer home in 1963, was where we celebrated lots of birthdays and anniversaries. After 1960, summer celebrations were usually at Fox Lake with picnics, outdoor grilling, swimming, and singing.

July 4, 1965, was Pop Spencer's ninetieth surprise birthday party at Fox Lake. Donald's father, Charles, was called "Pop," or sometimes "Firecracker," because of his July 4th birthday. Family members from Toledo; Washington, D.C.; Texas; Marysville, Ohio; Cincinnati; Seattle; and California all came to Fox Lake for that party—and other times. Pop was really surprised. He died suddenly at Fox Lake a few days later from a massive heart attack.

Thanksgiving was for extended family, like birthdays. It was a potluck, with everybody bringing something. I always made the cranberry sauce and Daddy brought the wine. We always played cards after dinner—whist, bridge, and canasta. Mother Spencer was a good card player but she didn't like to lose. The holidays are not the same, since so many of my generation are gone, but we still have lots of memories.

December 2014 marked the seventy-second year of our annual Christmas breakfast for family and close friends. Donald and I began the breakfast tradition when we first married. Mildred lives in Washington, D.C., but several times she and her family came. Camille Malcolm, Mildred's daughter, a UC graduate, lives in Cincinnati. She convinced me to continue to hold this important event even after Donald's death in 2010. My son Edward has come every year but one from California, and Donald Jr.'s son, Oliver, and his wife, Davina, comes from Seattle. We've always had between twenty and thirty-five guests each year. I often didn't get to bed on Christmas Eve. Lucky for me, I didn't have to worry about Christmas dinner, which was at Mother Spencer's as long as she could manage it. We just had Christmas dinner a few days later when Mother Spencer got older.

I have done all the cooking, and the menu has always been the same for the Christmas breakfasts. I have to start three days in advance to prepare the country ham. After it is braised, scored, and baked it takes a day to get cold for slicing Christmas morning. We always have scrambled eggs and hot yeast rolls that I make from scratch. Donald would always cut fruit to make a fresh fruit compote. The table is set with my good china and a beautiful centerpiece. Camille says if I will continue to make the ham she will prepare the rest for future years.

Donald celebrated his ninetieth birthday in 2005. It was really special. Donald had written three musical comedies when he was a student at UC, for which he was later given his honorary doctorate. For this birthday, over three hundred people were invited to a show in the Cincinnati Art Museum auditorium. Donald recruited his UC fraternity brothers, most of the cast from the old musicals he had written for the University Singers and Players and Quadres, and some of the original band. They rehearsed for weeks and played and sang many of Donald's original songs. Relatives from California and Washington, D.C., came. The show was a great hit, as much for the participants as for all who attended. Everybody had a memorable time.

I think the best of many celebrations was our fiftieth wedding anniversary, August 12, 1990. First, we had a separate extended family dinner at the Bankers Club. Then we invited more than five hundred family and friends for an open house at our home on Lexington Avenue. The day began at 9:00 a.m. at Mount Zion United

Methodist Church on Altoona Street, in Walnut Hills. Spencer family members filled two rows of pews. Then we had a "working lunch" so everybody could help get ready for the big party.

About seven hundred people came. They filled up the living room, dining room, kitchen, and terrace, and the kids played basketball in the driveway or Ping-Pong in the basement. It was a beautiful day, and the terrace outside and the house were filled with flowers. Our relatives came from all over the country: Donald's brother, Joseph, from California; his sister, Valerie, from St. Louis; Mildred and her family from Washington, D.C.; and many more. We had all the relatives wear a gold-ribbon boutonniere so people would know who was family. Governor Richard Celeste came, and many local politicians. The president of Ohio University, Dr. Charles Ping, and his wife flew down from Athens, Ohio.

Donald and I had eaten dinner at the five-star Maisonette restaurant downtown on other special occasions. We knew a young black assistant chef there. Donald spoke to the young man to ask if he [Donald] could afford to have the Maisonette cater the fiftieth-anniversary party. Our young friend said he wanted to cater the party, but we could not pay him. This young man came at 9:00 in the morning and stayed until 9:00 that night, and there was a continuous parade of delicious food the entire time.

In addition to the excellent and profuse amount of food, there was music all day. Our piano and organ were covered by Donald's sister Valerie, Billie Van Winkle, and others. Billie was the pianist at the Cincinnatian Hotel for many years. She used to call Donald or come to the house when she needed a bridge or transition between songs. She would play the piano and Donald would sit at the organ. Donald would work out any song she could sing, play a transition, or arrange a change of key. She would ask about a song someone had requested at the hotel that she didn't know, and Donald would play it for her. It was one of the best celebrations ever.

FAMILY TRAVELS—
AT HOME AND ABROAD

Donald had always wanted to travel. As a father and social studies teacher, he wanted to show his sons most of the forty-eight state capitol buildings (at that time), and many national parks. He also wanted to give his sons an idea of the vastness of the nation and bring back materials for his classes. They traveled during the summer when school was out for Donald and the boys.

The late 1940s and 1950s was the era of the Lincoln Highway (U.S. Route 40) and Route 66.[2] Early motels were often tiny "cottages" in a row behind the proprietor's home or office right next to the two-lane roads. Later, motels were built in one- or two-story rows of attached rooms, often with a swimming pool and nearby restaurants. There were no billboards, but sometimes a series of six or eight Burma Shave signs with amusing riddles were placed next to the road.[3]

Motels were independently owned and operated. Many proprietors restricted room rentals to whites or "suitable people." Signs in the motel and restaurant windows often stated, "We reserve the right to refuse service." If you were a black family traveling outside the South, you needed the Urban League's *Negro Motorist Green Book* in order to know which motels, restaurants, parks, and even whole towns would serve blacks.[4]

Marian's memory:

We took several summer vacations and visited forty-six states and many national parks when the kids were young. It was sometimes easier to travel in the South where it was clear what black families could and could not do, or where we could go. In the South, "Whites Only" and "Blacks Only" signs were prominent on restaurants, restrooms, water fountains, and motels and over the top of entrance doors in public buildings. The Urban League distributed a guide for black travelers listing by states and cities where Negroes could eat, or whether they needed to go to the back door of a restaurant to get carryout orders. The book also listed where you could find overnight accommodations or buy groceries. Service stations sold only gas and, maybe, candy bars and the local newspaper. They might, or might not, allow Negroes to use the restrooms. There were signs posted at the edge of towns all over the northern and midwestern states that said blacks had to be out of the town by sundown. If we were there after dark, we faced arrest or a police escort to the city limits.[5]

We would take two, sometimes three weeks, to travel while Daddy was not teaching. We had to have an ice chest with fruit, snacks, and drinks in the car because we never knew where we would be at lunchtime, or if we could find a restaurant that would serve us. Many roadside restaurants had a side window where blacks could order and pick up their food to eat outside on a picnic table, or we had to eat in the car. At these places, blacks were not allowed inside to use the restrooms. If there was not an old outhouse behind the restaurant, sometimes we were told "just go 'round back." We would drive about three hundred miles a day, for six or seven hours, and stop about 3:00 in the afternoon to make sure we had a clean place to spend the night, and to shower or swim to cool off before dinner. Air-conditioned cars came a lot later.

One of our first trips started with a visit to my twin, Mildred, and her family in Washington, D.C. Then we went south along the East Coast. We left Washington in midafternoon and drove into Maryland. We stopped at a restaurant along the highway for supper. There was a long wait after we were seated and served water. I could see the kitchen door and the waiter and kitchen crew were huddled together and glancing toward us. They couldn't tell if we were local Negroes or visiting diplomats. They could serve us if we were diplomats. We looked like we might be international visitors: we were nicely dressed and our family is several shades of black. Donald Jr. even has straight hair. After about twenty minutes, the manager came to our table and told us we had to leave. We did, but not before Daddy told the manager that some day he, the manager, would learn that Donald's money was just as green as anyone else's.

We stopped in Salt Lake City to see the Mormon Temple and hear the Mormon Tabernacle Choir on another trip to the Southwest. The first task in any town was to locate a place to stay overnight. The Urban League guide listed a motel where we could stay. The guide said if there were a vacancy sign, but we were refused service, we should form a line and have other customers line up behind us to wait their turn. I guess it just depended on who was at the registration desk whether or not they would rent to Negroes. There was a vacancy sign at 4:00 that afternoon, but we were told there were no more rooms. Donald said we would wait.

A line began to form outside behind us, perhaps five or six additional white people wanting rooms. When a white family with young children joined the queue, Don relented and told them to come ahead of him and get a room. The Canadian couple in line just behind us saw immediately what was happening. In a very loud voice the Canadian gentleman announced that if this place would not take Donald's money, they wouldn't get his either. Our family and the Canadians left the line to cross the road to a nearby bed-and-breakfast not listed in the guide. There we were greeted warmly by a woman with a strong foreign accent.

We all wanted to see the Tabernacle Choir that evening. Before we left to get dinner, however, our friendly bed-and-breakfast hostess told us that Negroes had to sit in the back rows in the balcony to hear the choir. I refused to go, but Donald took the boys for this unique experience, despite the discriminatory seating.

Once, and only once, did I allow myself to knowingly pass for white. You know, if one drop of black blood is so precious, I will claim every bit of it. We had been driving for hours and we had to stop during a heavy rainstorm. We got to the next town after it was dark. Donald told me to go into the motel office and get rooms, which I did. We had a good night's sleep.

The next morning the proprietor was astounded to see our black family walk into the lobby to pay our bill, get some coffee, and ask for ice for our ice chest. We received really fast service and were hustled out the door and on our way before other motel guests would see that a Negro family had been there overnight.

There was a later trip, when Donnie [Donald Jr.] was a young teenager, that I remember too well. Donnie liked to give Daddy [Donald Sr.] a hard time about the car. We had spent days rolling through the breadbasket of America, and Donnie kept complaining that if we had a V-8 engine, instead of a V-6, we could go faster and farther every day. We were near Albuquerque, New Mexico, when Daddy had had enough of this talk. He told Donnie that if he made anymore comments about the car he would have to get out and walk. I thought this was a terrible threat, but I didn't think anything would happen. Then Donnie did it again. Daddy stopped the car by the curb in the middle of Albuquerque. He told Donnie to get out. Donnie reached for his stash of personal money he had saved for souvenirs on the trip and got out of the car to stand on the curb. Daddy immediately drove off, turned left, and went around the block. When we got back to where Donnie had gotten out of the car he was not there! I began to cry. Daddy kept reassuring me we would find Donnie. Daddy went into all the buildings nearby asking whether anyone had seen our boy. They had not. I was really upset. Daddy began to drive slowly down the street. After several blocks we saw Donnie walking along the same direction we had been headed. After Donnie got back in the car, and I stopped crying, Daddy said it looked like Donnie had a plan. Donnie said, yes, he did. He was going to get a dishwashing job and earn enough money to buy a bus ticket home—home to

Aunt Millie's in Washington, D.C. I don't think we heard any-more complaints about the car.

I particularly loved the giant sequoias and redwood trees along the West Coast, but I was always glad to return home. We visited the Grand Canyon, Yosemite, Yellowstone, and Glacier National Parks, and each state capitol in the states we traveled through. I remember Donald telling the boys that these were not city parks. When he spoke the boys were to listen carefully, and under no circumstances were they to get too close to the edge of cliffs, the roaring waterfalls, or other hazardous places like bubbling mud pots and geysers. At Mount Rushmore, Donald told the boys there was nowhere else in the world where they would see anything like where the presidents are carved in stone on this scale. I kept a daily journal when we first started traveling. The kids loved to look back at their antics in the diary, but the recording became cumbersome and I quit doing it after a few years.

Later, after we were empty-nested, Donald wanted to see the world. I thought about going to law school because I thought it would help me implement change. Donald was afraid that if I became a lawyer I would not be able to take time off to travel because I would be too involved in my work. So I skipped the law degree but was always involved in improving something. We had a nearly ideal retirement that allowed us to travel and to support many causes, scholarships, and program initiatives.

For six years we traveled to Puerto Vallarta, Mexico, to use a timeshare we helped our son Edward and his wife, Priscilla, pur-chase. It was an enclave owned by Canadians that excluded much of the feel of visiting a foreign country. We did, however, learn of all the best restaurants and particularly enjoyed dinners while watching the sun set over the Pacific Ocean.

My dear friend Harriet Rauh, whom I followed as president of Fellowship House in the 1960s, was a travel agent. Harriet and her husband traveled first-class everywhere and she convinced me that we should do the same. She sent us to unusual places off the beaten path. Back then, in the 1960s and '70s, it was unusual for black Americans to travel abroad. We were treated with interest. Donald did not care for ship travel; he said he did not want to be on a boat where he could not swim to shore. We returned from Europe via ship just once.

I remember going to the first revolving restaurant I had ever seen in Japan. When we were in Greece, we stayed at the same hotel at the same time as a U.S. president, but I don't remember who that was. I was very impressed that the rooms had luxurious bathrobes, which was new to me then. My major impressions of China were the shocking latrines, the one-child government policy, the enormous number of bicycles, and the very rough train-track beds as we traveled to different parts of the country.

I was disturbed by the poor conditions and poverty in many places, particularly in Port-au-Prince, Haiti. Donald had selected a downtown hotel—this was long before there was an internet. The taxicab driver who picked us up at the airport would not let us out of the car at the hotel we had selected. He said he could not leave us in that area: it was unclean, dangerous, and we had no business there. So he took us to a tourist hotel on a hilltop above the city. At this hotel there were golden faucets, green marble baths, and a view of the ocean from three sides of the room. It was frequented primarily by white Americans who came there for three-day-weekend divorces. We stayed two weeks! There were parties at the hotel but only blacks from a high economic status could attend. The economic disparity was painfully obvious. Ownership of most of the better areas of the island was by foreigners who came primarily for their vacations.

I was surprised in the Caribbean islands and African countries. Somehow I didn't expect that the authorities would be people of color. Blacks performed every function that Caucasians did back home. These public servants were as effective and efficient as whites in other countries. Seems like we can make poor assumptions based on our own experiences, or lack thereof.

Barbados was very different from Haiti. Our good friend Sophia Carruthers had moved there from Cincinnati after she was widowed. Sophia and her husband, George, had been some of our bridge-playing friends in Cincinnati. At their home in Madeira, just outside Cincinnati, George suddenly became very ill and needed to be transported to a hospital. The ambulance was en route to General Hospital when George had a crisis. The ambulance stopped at the closest medical center, in the Village of Mariemont, a suburb on the east side of Cincinnati. The Mariemont medical center refused to admit George because he was black. They said take him on to General Hospital downtown. He died in transit to General, now University Hospital.

Mariemont was a planned community for working-class whites built in the 1920s by Mrs. Emery, wife of the founder of Cincinnati's Emery Industries.[6] Blacks and Jews were excluded. I was invited to give a talk to the Greater Cincinnati Foundation's Women's Fund in Mariemont in 2013. My friend Lois Rosenthal was also invited. Lois called me to ask if she should go: Lois is Jewish. Like me, she had never been inside this community except for once or twice going to the movie theater there. I told her to definitely come, bring her husband, and sit in the first row. I started off my speech telling the audience why the Rosenthals and I had never before been in a community building in Mariemont. The young women there were really surprised by my story. They didn't know Cincinnati surrounds, and is surrounded by, several small cities —sundown towns—built exclusively for whites.

After George Carruthers' untimely death from meningitis, Sophia moved to Barbados. Later she remarried. Donald and I went to visit her there. The local church in Barbados had a fabulous organ played by a talented organist. There was a huge church, which during the week looked to be much too large for the population. It was filled on Sundays. It seemed everyone on the island must have come to hear and enjoy the church music. We visited Sophia twice. Her house had been built by an English sea captain. The downstairs housed the bedrooms and the living areas were on the second floor. From the wraparound windows on the second floor there was a full view of the ocean. You could watch the sun rise and set from the same spot inside the house. Sophia was the only African American in her economic class on the island but she organized an ongoing bridge club among all her international neighbors.

It was easier for me to relate to European culture than to the islands or Africa. In Europe I could predict what was expected of us as visitors. I think because we traveled first-class, we didn't have any discrimination problems. Wherever we went, we enjoyed the experience and the comparisons to home. Some of the countries we visited had a few advantages over the United States, but I could work for change back home.

Donald was president of the Board of Trustees of Ohio University (OU) in 1978. The university sent us to Kuala Lumpur to confer graduate degrees on students at the OU program there. Donald and I received honorary doctorates from Ohio University in 2008. But on that trip I felt like we were treated like royalty. One of our stops in transit was Hong Kong. At that time, mainland China was not open to foreign tourists.

Donald wanted to see the Panama Canal even though he did not like ship travel. He was sure the ship would not be too far at sea and that, if necessary, he could swim to shore. Our grandson Oliver and his wife, Davina, met us on the dock in Florida to send us off. It was a first-class trip all the way.

We watched a film about the building of the canal on board the ship to Panama from Florida. I was appalled that so many people had died in the process of this building project. Many of the deaths were from malaria, and, they said, up until then, it was the largest ever earth-moving project in the world. When we got to the canal, there was very little space between the ship's side and the locks. Coming the opposite direction, going east, were ships from China and many other places bringing goods to the United States.

I loved that trip; it was elegant. There were flowers in the stateroom, candy on the pillow, even spirits in the bottles in the room. There were about four staff to each passenger—somebody at our elbow all the time. The food was delicious, and it was great fun to eat at the captain's table. In the three or four days it took to go through the canal, there was always something to do. There were evening shows and even someone to teach bridge lessons—which of course we didn't need.

There was a picnic on shore one day. Everyone took a small boat from the side of the ship. We were served caviar and drinks before lunch—the waiters wading in the water to serve passengers on the beach or floating out on the water. It was probably the most expensive trip we ever took, but it was fabulous. The experience was unique—our last trip abroad together. There are twenty-two countries stamped on our passports, beginning in India in 1965. Even though I went around the world three times, I was always glad to return home.

FOX LAKE

Daddy and I looked for integrated summer camps and programs for the boys. We weren't going to spend money to send the kids to a segregated camp. The boys did attend a camping program at Camp Joy just outside Cincinnati, where Rev. Maurice McCrackin made sure all children were welcome.[7] Mac McCrackin became a close friend of the family and role model for Donnie and Edward. He lost his job as director of Camp Joy primarily because he insisted on integrating the program.

We tried two other integrated summer camps, one down South and another in New England, before we discovered Fox Lake, near Angola, Indiana.[8] Fox Lake is a registered Historical National Resort.[9] It was built as an African American resort; I think there are only two or three in the country. The property adjoined a large farm. Forty-foot lots were partitioned off surrounding Fox Lake. For several summers after 1950, we rented a cabin each summer, and in 1963 we bought three lots and built a summer home at the lake.

Daddy and the boys swam every day at Fox Lake. I couldn't swim before 1949. I would stand on the shore with Jockimo and be convinced that they would all drown. We had a Fox Lake Swim Club with a lifeguard and the boys earned the rank of Shark when they could swim the mile-length of the lake and back. The girls had to swim across the lake and back, about three-quarters of a mile each way, in order to be called Sharkettes. I thought our boys were part fish. The kids always liked summers at Fox Lake when the family was all together and work was left behind.

Many African American teachers, mostly from Indianapolis, built summer homes there. Donald became president of the Fox Lake Property Owners' Association. He led the fundraising and supervised the building of a lakeside lodge for the organization. Several nationally prominent black musicians took detours from Chicago to perform at Fox Lake. I have been on the board of trustees since 2010. I still go to the lake for two months every summer. Ever since Donald died, if I don't get to the lake by July 4, I start to get calls from the neighbors there asking when I will arrive. I can't get away with anything!

After our Fox Lake vacation in 1949, I decided I needed to learn to swim. Back home in Cincinnati, I went to the Norwood YWCA and took lessons from a YW staff member.[10] It was the year the national YW adopted my resolution to desegregate their swimming pools all across the country.

One day I was swimming laps and the Norwood YW director began walking slowly alongside the pool, keeping even with my pace. I kept on swimming and ignored her. The director knew me; she knew I had been president of the black West End YWCA and that I was currently vice president of the board of directors at the Metropolitan YWCA. She probably knew that I was responsible for the new mandatory desegregation of YW pools. Finally the director gave up. She had to waste about half-an-hour of her time walking up and down by the pool. It was clear that the Norwood YW needed work on desegregation. I never went to swim at the Williams YMCA on McMillan Street in Cincinnati, even though it was walking distance from my home. I was never comfortable there. They remained segregated for a long time.[11]

Whenever we were at Fox Lake, after I learned to swim, Donald and I would swim across the lake and back before breakfast every morning. Some time after we were both over eighty, we swam only to the middle of the lake before turning back. In August 2012, I was swimming at the lake when two Tuskegee airmen, flying restored Red Tail planes that had escorted World War II bombers over Europe, did a flyover. They dipped their wings to acknowledge the resort before landing at the small Angola airfield. There was a three-day celebration honoring the Tuskegee Airmen. A local man from Madisonville, John Leahr, was a brave member of the World War II Tuskegee Airmen heroes.

One summer at Fox Lake in the 1970s, when our grandsons, Matthew, then seventeen, and Oliver, sixteen, were visiting, a KKK march was scheduled in the town of Angola, just a few miles away. I took the boys to see it. Students from the local Tryne College protested the march. They got the people in Angola to close their doors and draw their window curtains. If people were on the street they turned their backs on the KKK marchers. There was no violence. I was glad to take my grandsons to see this and to recall for them my experience watching the KKK as a child. Oliver, now a lawyer in Seattle, said he would never forget it.

People have asked how we managed to raise a family with all the civic and social justice work Donald and I have always done. And they give me credit for being cheerful almost all the time. Well, I tried being grumpy; cheerful works better.

Donald and I had different but effective methods of handling anger or discipline when it came to the children. My family was pretty volatile when I was growing up. If somebody was angry, everybody knew it. My brother Harry had a real temper and got in trouble for socking another student for a racial slur. Once he even knocked out somebody's teeth. I would "fly off" sometimes. When I was young, I would even throw something if I were really mad. More often I would march outside and slam the door. I didn't throw anything after I grew up, but I was known to stalk outside and bang the door sometimes.

It wasn't like that with Donald. The first time I got really angry after we were married, I wanted to pound on Donald's chest. He calmly took my arms and said we couldn't fight physically. If we did, the marriage wouldn't last. That set the tone for us, and how we approached discipline with the boys. It was always acceptable to say what you thought, as long as you were respectful, but it was not acceptable to get physical about it. Donald would think about what he wanted to say for several minutes before speaking if he were angry with someone outside the family. If it were something important to say to our sons, he might think about it for a couple of days. With me, Donald said it was pretty hard to stay mad if you prayed together every night.

We wrote a family contract that all four of us signed when the boys started driving. Daddy had agreed to pay half the cost of a used car for each of them if the boys paid the other half from money they had earned. This contract said: none of us would go out of town without giving notice; nobody else would drive the boys' cars; and no one would drink and drive. I remember once one of the boys' car distributor caps was on Daddy's dresser for a while until Daddy decided the proper lesson had been learned about safe driving. One time a cab driver was talking about teen discipline with Donald. The cabbie said he would never sign a contract like that with his parents. Donald replied: "You are not my son."

We didn't yell or fight with each other, or with the boys. I did scold and discipline the boys at the time they did something wrong; I didn't wait for Daddy to get home. I think I only used a switch off the apple tree twice—both times it was when the kids were very young and did something that jeopardized their safety, like playing in the street. When Daddy was angry or upset he would sit down at the piano and keep playing until he felt better. He played the piano or organ every day. You could tell his mood by how he played.

We were a good team. We supported each other in whatever tasks each chose. We prayed together every night for strength to keep on working for needed change. We made music together for seventy years.

The 1950s were quickly consumed by family life at the Spencers'; Marian's Coney Island lawsuit in 1952; a move to the new house in 1953; summer travels across the country; and, as documented by Marian's datebooks for each year, continuing work with the NAACP, the Charter Committee, and the YWCA. She was also a new member of the Woman's City Club.

Marian:

The year after Coney Island, in 1953, Donald Jr. passed the entrance exam to attend Walnut Hills High School. He had been attending Douglass School, which went to the eighth grade. The Douglass School principal wanted to keep him there. I felt Donnie should have the advantages of Walnut Hills High School since he had passed the exam.[12] After politely, but unsuccessfully, asking that Donnie be transferred, I kept Donnie out of school for two weeks in protest. Finally, the superintendent of schools called me to tell me I had to send Donnie to school. The superintendent agreed about Walnut Hills High School and said he would oversee the transfer of records. Apparently the Douglass principal wanted Donnie to stay in order to stop all the smart kids from transferring out of his school.

Later my full attention was diverted from my civic work because of Edward's accident. Edward was fourteen and attending Walnut Hills High School in 1956. One day there was a terrible accident at an after-school football game. The coach brought Edward home because there was some question about after-school insurance for athletes. Edward's neck was tilted awkwardly. I immediately called our neighbor, Dr. Clark, to come look at Edward. Dr. Clark asked Edward to raise his arm, which he did, and it immediately flopped back down. Dr. Clark said to meet him at the nearby Jewish Hospital in ten minutes.[13] Edward was in such pain at the hospital they put him on a gurney and cut his clothes off. Edward told me that his legs flopped just like his arm had. I said, "We'll take care of it."

Edward's neck was broken. His fourth and fifth vertebrae were involved—one fractured, one dislocated. Edward's claim to fame was that his injury was the same as that of the Brooklyn Dodgers' catcher, Roy Campanella.

Nine months later, after the fracture had healed, the dislocated vertebra had to be surgically realigned. It was unclear whether Edward might be a quadriplegic. The orthopedic doctor told me, "I can promise you nothing." The neurosurgeon said he had every faith that Edward would fully recover. Daddy (Donald Sr.) had the flu at the time of the surgery to put the dislocated vertebra back in place. He could not go to the hospital. He wrote Edward a beautiful letter that I took to the hospital and read to Edward that morning. Edward told me to place the letter in a drawer near his bed and read it to him again when he returned from the operation. Uncle Mac, my brother, accompanied me to Jewish Hospital, where the operation was performed.

Edward's temperament was extraordinary. All the kids called out to wish him luck as the hospital staff wheeled Edward out of the juvenile ward for surgery. With remarkable cheer, Edward told his Uncle Mac, "Be careful with the traction pulleys. If you catch them on the elevator door you'll break my neck." His classmates from Walnut Hills High School all signed a small figure and sent it to him. Many visited Edward over his three-month stay at the hospital.

My friend Patricia Collins was a nurse at Jewish Hospital. She described the operation to reposition the dislocated vertebra. Edward, unconscious, was suspended vertically from the ceiling in traction. The doctor stood behind him for the entire surgery. Edward's operation was so delicate the doctor took a full week off work to recover from the effort.

For four months after the accident, Edward had been horizontal and always in traction. I was at Edward's bedside in the hospital every day and for many nights, particularly right after the surgery. I slept in Edward's hospital room to insure that his covers did not slip off. The doctors said if Edward caught a cold or pneumonia he would die. Dr. Chester Pierce, a psychiatrist friend and former renter from us on Burdett Avenue, was an intern at Jewish Hospital. He came by the room after the surgery to read Edward's chart. Clearly, Edward was depressed. Dr. Pierce took Daddy out of the room and said, "Go get him some girlie books." I never knew what books or magazines Donald provided, but it helped turn Edward around.

Our family friend Oscar Robertson visited Edward and brought him a basketball. The University of Cincinnati basketball coach had brought Oscar to us the previous year when the coach feared that Oscar was homesick and might not stay in Cincinnati. We all became good friends. Edward said, "Put the ball in the back of the closet. I'll never play basketball again." I said, "Oh yes you will."

The doctors disagreed about whether Edward should go home for Christmas. The neurologist wanted him to remain in the hospital and the orthopedic doctor thought Edward should go home for psychological reasons. Edward was put in a full-body cast, with only his face and arms uncovered. The cast weighed more than he did. He could move by rocking himself to a sitting position and, with help, he could stand. The doctor said if he fell and broke the cast his neck would be broken again.

The first Sunday morning after Edward was home his friends from church came at 6:00 to sing Christmas carols outside Edward's bedroom window. Edward didn't want his friends to see him in traction and his cast, but I said he had to greet them through his bedroom window since they had made such an effort to come. He stood to wave to them. It was an important turning point in his recovery. Edward did make a full recovery; he just could no longer play basketball or dive when swimming. Everybody rejoiced, and life got back to normal.

Both our boys attended Syracuse University. Just two weeks before Donald Jr.'s planned Syracuse graduation in 1962, we experienced another family crisis. Our son Donald had a severe breakdown. Daddy and I drove all night to get to Syracuse, New York. When we went to pick him up, I remember the school dean said Donald needed to get off campus immediately. The dean also said that nearly every week parents had to come to rescue students who were overwhelmed by the pressure to succeed. We brought Donald home and it was some time before he recovered. Don Jr. had enough credits to receive his undergrad degree with his class from Syracuse and he made a full recovery. Later, Donald went on to Atlanta University and obtained a master's degree in library science.

Donald Jr. became a Cincinnati Public School librarian and is now retired. He married and has three children—Benita, Matthew, and Oliver— and one grandson, Benita's son, Emmanuel Brockman. Edward finished college and did graduate work at the Ohio State University. He undertook additional specialist training and now has a holistic medicine and acupuncture practice in Richmond, California. He married Priscilla Regalado. They do not have any children.

When Donald Jr.'s son Oliver was twelve and his parents divorced, he asked to move in with us. His mother allowed him to do so when he was fourteen. We became parents again as Oliver moved in. Oliver graduated from Walnut Hills High School four years later and completed college and law school. He is now a practicing attorney in Seattle, Washington. Oliver's older brother, Matthew, is autistic and lives with his mother in Indianapolis. Emmanuel, my great-grandson, is a 2013 honor graduate from Princeton High School in suburban Cincinnati, where he placed first in Ohio and fourth in the nation in a computer technology competition in his senior year. He has a full scholarship to attend Cincinnati State College, where he started in September 2013.

IV

Desegregation Suits and
Continuing Battles

CONEY ISLAND

O HIO GROVE, the "Coney Island of the West," opened June 21, 1886, just ten miles up river from Cincinnati.[1] That summer, the steamboat Guiding Star made runs to the park four times a day. A fifty-cent round-trip ticket included park admission. The name Ohio Grove was dropped in 1887, and the park became known simply as Coney Island. In 1889, a new company, the Coney Island Company, took over the park. The buyers were led by Commodore Lee Brooks, who got his start selling tickets on riverboats and made a fortune in tobacco, retail, trolleys, and steamboats.[2]

The new owners continued to be as successful as the original operator and purchased neighboring farms to expand the park. One of Coney Island's landmark features, Lake Como, named for a famous lake in Italy, was purchased in 1893. The lake, located a short distance from the river in a former cornfield, became the focal point for many of the park's early amusements, such as the Giant Circle Swing, Shoot the Chutes, and rowboats. The park became a regional attraction—a respite every summer from the hot, crowded streets of Cincinnati. The hour-long boat ride from Cincinnati's public landing to the park, which lasted until the Island Queen burned in 1957, originally cost ten cents.

Coney Island amusement park, including Lake Como, Moonlight Gardens dance hall, and the large Sunlite swimming pool, prospered. Like most of the country's public city park programs and pools, golf courses, clubs, and other sources of entertainment, the park was segregated.

Marian's experience:

I never paid any attention to Coney Island in Cincinnati because I knew we couldn't go there. Then one day in 1952, my boys were watching the popular "Uncle Al" television program for children. Uncle Al was showing the lake with paddleboats, the merry-go-round, roller coaster, and other rides. "Everybody come to Coney Island!" Uncle Al said. Edward and Donald Jr. were eight and ten years old, and they said they wanted to go, too. I thought I knew what the answer would be, but I decided to check.

I went to the kitchen, so the boys would not hear me, and I called Coney Island amusement park. The girl who answered the park phone said of course the boys would be welcome until I said, "but we're Negroes." After a pause the girl said she was sorry, she didn't make the rules, but my children would not be allowed in the park. I told the girl I knew the office personnel didn't make that decision, but I would find out who did. My boys should be treated equally to any other children. It made me mad.

I was chair of the NAACP Legislative Committee that year and I decided the NAACP should desegregate this park. I called a meeting of all the local black lawyers, most of whom were members of the NAACP, to meet in the Manse Hotel ballroom, on Chapel Street in Walnut Hills. I told the group the NAACP would need legal counsel to sue Coney Island to stop segregation. The lawyers' response was that Ted Berry, the well-known civil rights lawyer, who was not present, should take the job. I knew that Ted was already too busy and I asked for someone to step forward. No one did. Later, privately, I confronted Micky Turpeau, the brother of my Laurel Homes friend Florida Turpeau Anderson, who was at the meeting. He quietly said he would file the suit and serve as legal counsel.

We had protest marches at the main gate to Coney Island. It was August and very hot. The police took pictures of the marchers, which included several well-dressed white women, some wearing hats and gloves. The national NAACP had told us we needed an integrated effort. The police took their pictures to Cincinnati Mayor Dot Dolbey to ask who the white women were at the gate. Mrs. Dolbey declined to identify the women, even though she knew them all. Most were members of the Woman's City Club, which had just opened its doors to Negro women. An integrated group of ministers drove to the front gate and got pelted with tomatoes, dirt clods, and fruit. Rev. McCrackin was slightly injured when somebody broke the car window on the passenger side of the car where he was sitting.

Several demonstrators were arrested and taken to jail, including Rev. McCrackin. They took those arrested to the Clermont County jail, instead of the old Cincinnati Workhouse, because public feeling about the demonstrations was pretty high. The police didn't want trouble at the jail. Rev. McCrackin and some others went on a hunger strike. They were released after a few days because there was real concern the protesters would become dehydrated and Rev. McCrackin could possibly die in the extreme heat. I remember when Donald and I went up to help bring them back when they were released.

Mr. Turpeau won the Coney Island antisegregation case at great personal cost. He was no longer able to get enough legal work to support a family in Cincinnati. He and his wife moved to Washington, D.C., so he could earn a living.

The Coney Island entrance gates and park were successfully desegregated. Blacks could picnic and ride the paddleboats and amusement rides because they are located in Hamilton County. The park's unique Sunlite Pool remained off limits to us for another eight years. The pool is physically situated in Clermont County. The lawsuit was filed in Hamilton County Court, so a separate legal action was needed for Clermont County. My neighbors, Dr. Bruce Green, his wife Lucy, and Abe Goldhagen, continued the fight to desegregate the pool. Finally, in 1961, the Sunlite Pool was opened to Negroes. I heard the real reason the pool opened was because the Cincinnati mayor wouldn't sign a business license renewal with Coney Island Corporation unless they desegregated the pool. I didn't want to go to the Sunlite Pool even though I had learned to swim.

SCHOOL SEGREGATION

The Ohio legislature authorized separate public schools for African Americans in 1849. Black schools were firmly established in Cincinnati under the direction of black trustees, elected by black taxpayers, and financed by a special tax on black-owned property by 1857.[3] Black property owners in Cincinnati also paid the local property tax that supported the white schools. In 1866 in Cincinnati, under the leadership of Peter H. Clark,[4] the black trustees established Gaines High School with grades seven to twelve, the first public high school of its kind in Ohio. The school was located at Clark and John Streets, just two blocks west of City Hall. A Normal (teaching) department was established in 1868. Virtually all the black teachers in southwestern Ohio were trained at Gaines High over the next twenty years. The Gaines graduates took the same accreditation exams as white teachers and their marks were comparable. Gaines High School was nationally recognized for its excellence.

The Ohio law mandating separate black schools was challenged in 1873 when the country was in a severe recession. Local Republicans wanted to make black schools optional and have a single school system run by a single elected board. This was accomplished by 1874. Cincinnati's single school board was elected; it was all-white.[5] Mixed schools became a hot political issue in Cincinnati primarily because black and white students were taught together, but only white teachers could teach in the mixed schools. There was an unwritten rule that black teachers would not teach white students.

Peter Clark, founder and principal of Gaines High School, was in favor of mixed schools, provided that the black and white teaching staffs were mixed as well as the students. Clark helped defeat the mixed school law in 1884.[6] The all-white Cincinnati School Board fired Peter Clark in 1886 because of Clark's opposition to the mixed schools law and his support of Democratic gubernatorial candidate George Hoadley. Clark was "too political." The mixed-school law to integrate students, but not teachers, passed again the following year. In 1887, the Arnett Act abolished segregated public schools in Ohio. Gaines High School was closed in 1889. An estimated eight hundred black children were placed in previously all-white schools by 1890.[7] One hundred and fifty-eight black students had graduated from Gaines, constituting much of Cincinnati's black middle class. Cincinnati's two remaining high schools, Hughes and Woodward, graduated only eighty-nine black students during the next twenty years despite the school-age black population having doubled during the period. The declining black student enrollment was attributed to a general lack of acceptance by white faculty and students, and low teacher expectations of black students. Cincinnati's elementary and junior high schools were well on their way to complete resegregation by the turn of the twentieth century.

The total economic, social, and political marginalization of blacks from mainstream society in Cincinnati was established by 1920. Students attended schools in their immediate (segregated) neighborhoods, thus accomplishing segregation despite the law. The school board built the excellent all-black K-9 Harriet Beecher Stowe School for Dr. Jennie Porter, the first black female Ph.D. from the University of Cincinnati. Not until 1943, however, was one black teacher assigned to a white Cincinnati public school. A second brave soul became a black teacher in a white elementary school in 1949.

In the decade from 1940 to 1950, including the war years, the Cincinnati black population went from 55,500 to 75,000, an increase of 40 percent.[8] By 1960, the black population was 108,757, or 39 percent of the total number of city residents. By 1970, the city lost 50,000 people, 95 percent of them white. Cincinnati had experienced a major shift in population: it was blacker and poorer.[9] The city's public schools went through a similar change. In addition to white flight to the suburbs, white families who could not, or who chose not to, move out of the city transferred thousands of children out of Cincinnati's public schools as the black population increased.[10] Catholic and private schools, both religious and secular, flourished.[11]

Following the 1954 *Brown v. Board of Education* U.S. Supreme Court decision that abolished separate but equal schools, the Cincinnati Public School (CPS) Board of Education and the Cincinnati branch of the NAACP began a long struggle to resolve issues that had not been addressed successfully since Reconstruction. CPS did not, however, establish policies to integrate the schools until 1972. That year a more liberal CPS Board passed a hotly contested comprehensive desegregation plan at the end of the year.[12] The intent was to insure a quality integrated education for all students in all Cincinnati public schools and to implement racial balance among teachers and students.

Marian Spencer was chair of the NAACP Education Committee in 1972. She had been attending the monthly CPS Board meetings to see what steps they intended to take to integrate Cincinnati's mostly segregated schools. At that time, school buses took black children to predominantly black schools even when there was a closer public school in a mostly white neighborhood. Black teenagers from "hilltop" Clifton and Avondale were bussed downtown to the West End's Taft High School, right past the doors of the elegant Hughes High School across the street from the University of Cincinnati.

Marian tells of her involvement:

Our local legal fight to improve school integration began back in the 1970s, or earlier. I attended the Cincinnati Public School Board meetings regularly. You could say I was a pain in the neck to the board president, Virginia Griffin. My primary complaint was the lack of any plan or progress to integrate Cincinnati schools following the *Brown v. Board of Education* decision. Mrs. Griffin's attitude was that the board was not doing anything to impede integration. Mrs. Griffin went so far as to advise my friend Marianna Brown Bettman, a future judge and law professor, not to sit with me at school board meetings as it could damage Ms. Bettman's reputation! Marianna and I had become friends through Fellowship House. Our work to integrate Cincinnati's public schools became a very long, discouraging process.

I ran for election to the CPS Board in 1973 because I wanted to implement the new integration plan adopted the year before. I was the first black female candidate to run for election to the Cincinnati school board. The liberal members of the board were up for reelection and we ran a hard, vigorous campaign. But we were defeated. A majority of voters didn't like the busing that was part of the desegregation plan adopted in December 1972. The newly elected conservative board voted to drop the previously approved plan. Four months later we (NAACP) filed the class action *Mona Bronson et al. v. Cincinnati Board of Education* lawsuit.

Donald and I were among several plaintiffs in the *Bronson* case. The purpose was to force implementation of the 1972 comprehensive integration plan that the newly elected board had overturned.

The lawsuit sought to assign staff to each school according to the racial balance of the district and included a busing plan. Initially, all the suburban school districts were included as codefendants along with the Ohio Department of Education. We included the white suburban districts, hoping for regional balance. The suburban school districts fought this in court, and they were allowed to pull out.

The NAACP and CPS also contested in court whether examples of Cincinnati school discriminatory practices that had been included in an earlier [discrimination] suit could be used by the NAACP in the *Bronson* case.[13] There were so many delays in the lawsuit and white flight kept getting worse. Even the argument that a consolidated school district would be more cost-effective and efficient didn't work. There are still more than twenty separate districts in the county.

The newspapers reported all the continuing trial delays of the case. School board candidates were allowed to discuss the case during the election campaign in 1977.[14] I was quoted in one *Cincinnati Enquirer* article regarding the indefinite postponement.[15] This article says:

> Marian Spencer, chairman of the local NAACP Education Committee, said "our lawyers told us this [the postponement] probably would occur. We hope it's short-lived." Spencer said she "hopes the judge who will get the case is a person who has a bit of experience in this area. I hope the judge who gets it is worthy of the case because it affects a lot of children, black and white."

You know the *Bronson* case never came to trial. The Court mandated establishment of the *Bronson* committee in 1984 to monitor progress of the court-ordered integration plan for the schools. I was asked to chair the committee but I wanted to be able to speak out about my opinions and not be restrained as the chair. This settlement even made the *New York Times*.[16] The settlement may have been a model but it was weak compared to the original lawsuit. We met, the *Bronson* committee, over the next twenty years, until 2004, to oversee the required changes in Cincinnati schools.

This case was the most frustrating of all the projects I've ever worked on. The delays took years. When the suburban districts were dismissed it gutted the whole thing. The magnet schools and integration of teachers were successes, and school busing was implemented, but the demographics of the whole city changed after 1960. White families just moved out or sent their kids to private schools. School segregation still continues as now children of African American and poor families are the majority attending public schools. The old housing patterns still mean that a majority of public schools are mostly segregated. That *Post* article about population shifts is still relevant today.[17]

We tried hard, but my philosophy has always been not to waste too much time looking back. There is too much left to do to lament what didn't work. We didn't lose the case for lack of trying. Looking back should be just long enough to see what lessons you can learn from a disappointment. I learned not to take defeat personally, from the school board election, the lengthy *Bronson* case, or reelection to city council. Sometimes, though, it is worth noting that even losing educates some people about the problem, and it is fun to think back about some of the victories.

CINCINNATI CITY COUNCIL

The *Cincinnati Post* ran a series of articles in 1980 showing that Cincinnati was the cancer capital of the United States.[18] There were city maps with overlays of where cancer cases were concentrated, invariably in low-income and minority neighborhoods, those near, or in the heart of, industrial activity. City council held a series of public hearings. It became clear that local citizens who lived near plants and the employees who worked around or handled toxic materials were totally unaware of carcinogenic materials being used in their midst. Firemen noted their serious personal risk when they responded to emergency incidents without advance notice of what materials might be burning, leaking, or perhaps exploding.

Dr. Eula Bingham, a former University of Cincinnati faculty member and former head of the Occupational Safety and Health Administration (OSHA) under President Carter, had returned to Cincinnati from Washington, D.C. She had tried unsuccessfully to establish Federal OSHA standards and Right-to-Know legislation. Dr. Bingham advised city council to pass a local Right-to-Know ordinance. All the large local corporations and the Chamber of Commerce were fiercely opposed.

Brewster Rhoads, then an employee of Ohio Citizen Action, offered to organize and staff a coalition to mount a major campaign for a local Right-to-Know ordinance if one or more well-known and highly respected leaders would chair the effort. Marian Spencer and the Rev. Fred Shuttlesworth, a veteran of the civil rights movement and close colleague of Martin Luther King Jr., agreed to cochair this effort. Hundreds of civil rights activists were drawn in to help, simply because people, both black and white, wanted to be associated with and work with these two prominent civil libertarians. This was clearly both a civil rights and an environmental issue.

Marian talks about her role:

The Right-to-Know campaign had volunteers go door-to-door with petitions to city council and educational materials. We organized telephone banks, poster campaigns, and a speaker's bureau. We recruited religious leaders, particularly in the African American churches. Unions, led by the firefighters, joined in and we got the Sierra Club and other environmental groups involved.

The Charter Committee finally noticed the broad support Rev. Shuttlesworth and I had built and they asked me to run for a seat on the Cincinnati City Council. I thought it was about time they asked—where had they been? I had been ready to run for council since the kids were out of high school. I had been waiting for Charter to ask me for several years. Maybe I was too polite to step forward and ask for support for election. But they finally asked and I joined the 1983 Charter Committee slate with former Mayor Bobbie Sterne and Charter incumbents Arnold Bortz and Tom Brush.

Brewster Rhoads and my husband, Donald, ran my city council campaign. Roxanne Qualls was another staff member of Ohio Citizen Action and she also worked on my campaign. Donald permanently closed his real estate business to do all he could to help me win.

One morning that September 1983, just two months before the election, Donald had every black minister in town come to breakfast on the terrace at our home. He told them that I needed their help to win. Rev. Wilbur Page, from Union Baptist, was there too. I had him baptize me and joined his church when I was a student at the University of Cincinnati forty years before this election. I told him I recognized his loyalty to the Republican Party, but I was a Charterite. There was no Democratic or Republican way to fix a pothole in the city, or to do something about hazardous materials and waste. The Charter Committee was independent; it was about good nonpartisan government. And I expected his support.

I don't remember where I ranked among the top nine candidates, but it was a thrill to get elected. All four Charter candidates won election. Tom Brush had made Right-to-Know legislation the single most important issue of his reelection campaign. Based on getting the top number of votes, he became mayor of Cincinnati in 1983. I was pleased to be the first African American woman elected to Cincinnati City Council.

I set up my city council office and hired Teri Reid and Roxanne Qualls as my council aides. The future Mayor Qualls began her career in politics with me. Roxanne was amazing; she covered every floor and even the basement in City Hall to learn exactly how the city operated. Roxanne became a "pro" at knowing how to get needed legislation passed, and she made me look good to city staff members because she cared about what work they were doing. She stayed with me for just a year, but we both learned a lot and got a lot done.

I chaired city council's law and development committees, and was council's representative on the City Planning Commission. The corporate community was so determined to stop Right-to-Know legislation that they didn't show up at meetings to draft the ordinance. As a result, we passed a strong ordinance. I was surprised that the ordinance received national attention and became the model for laws in Akron, Cleveland, and Columbus. Then Right-to-Know became statewide legislation in Ohio. The Federal Superfund legislation to fund toxic waste cleanup was due for renewal in 1985 and Right-to-Know language was attached, based on the Cincinnati ordinance.

My second year on council I was appointed vice mayor by Mayor Arnold Bortz. Council member and former mayor Bobbie Sterne was my primary mentor. I also often consulted with Council Clerk Webster Posey. I had known Web for years as a member of Theodore Berry's law firm. He was very helpful if I had a procedural question or simply needed advice about council matters. Bobbie Sterne helped me understand details so I could support her efforts regarding funding for human services and equal opportunity employment. Another major issue in 1984 was expansion of the Metro bus transit system. Like today, many workers, particularly blacks, didn't own cars and they needed good bus service to get to work.

I got into a little trouble my second year in office. I have this *Cincinnati Enquirer* article, including my picture, headed: "Spencer's Study of Communities Called Political."[19] I spent $2,500 of my council office budget to hire a local nonprofit consultant firm to create a profile of each neighborhood in the city. I wanted current, useful information readily available. One of my campaign goals had been to improve neighborhoods. We needed demographics, income levels, and information about community councils. Republican council member Guy Guckenberger and Democrat Ken Blackwell criticized the report, calling it an unusual expenditure for an individual council member that "smacks of using public dollars for political purposes." Clearly, I thought the expenditure was appropriate, and, fortunately, the city solicitor agreed it was legal. The other council members probably didn't like the report because they didn't think to do it themselves or because the front cover said "Provided by Marian Spencer, Council Member, City of Cincinnati." The report pulled together census statistics, issues facing each community based on interviews of community leaders, and a matrix of neighborhood characteristics. I was just doing my job!

I really enjoyed being on city council. I felt the law committee was an important assignment because there we could make real change. Council was supposed to be a part-time job but I also attended neighborhood community council meetings in the evening —and there are fifty-two separate neighborhoods—and I served on the City Planning Commission. I was busy, but it was fun.

The Christmas I was vice mayor I was assigned to give a city proclamation at the opening of the annual Salvation Army Christmas Toy Store. One of my friends at the Salvation Army reminded me of a story back then.

The ladies of the Salvation Army Toy Store Auxiliary make a big deal on the first day of toy shopping by many poor families. The fully uniformed Salvation Army band played Christmas carols over and over and the day's six hundred selected families waited for their opportunity to "shop" among the ten thousand new toys. The Colonel prayed, the band played, and they cut the ribbon.

Then I read the city proclamation. After that I went into the waiting room to speak to the mothers who were excited to be able to get gifts for their children. The shopping room wasn't big enough for them all to shop at once. Two of the mothers whispered to each other: "Which politician is she . . . she's got to be Governor Martha Layne Collins [KY], isn't she?" Governor Collins was blonde, blue-eyed, and much taller than me, but it made me smile.

I took every opportunity I could to tell everyone to vote. I have never missed a primary vote or general election. One cold winter day I went to the food stamp office where people had to line up for recertification for food stamps. I had a clipboard and voter registration cards from the League of Women Voters. I shook hands along the waiting line and encouraged these folks to be sure to register to vote. Sometimes I traded my clipboard to hold their babies so they could complete the voter registration forms. It seemed strange that people said, "What are you doing out here in the cold?" I was doing my job!

I lost reelection in 1985. It was a huge disappointment for me and all my supporters. We had worked very hard. It was a bad city council election for all three women on council—Charterites and Democrats. Sally Fellerhoff, a Democrat, was the other first-time city council member, and even the council veteran Bobbie Sterne lost. There was a major Republican sweep of offices—local, state, and nationwide. I've been told I also lost some of my environmental supporters who thought I was too pro-development on the Planning Commission and development committee. A *Cincinnati Enquirer* editorial cartoon by Jim Borgman, just after the election, showed the new, all-male, Republican-majority city council in a tree house pulling up the ladder. The caption read "No Girls Allowed."[20]

FAIR HOUSING

The 1964 Civil Rights Act slowly opened the door for minorities to live in any neighborhood of their choice. It was a hard sell in northern cities with a sizable number of minority residents. The law required landlords and real estate agents to stop discriminating against anyone who qualified financially for housing in any neighborhood. In Cincinnati, this often meant that many vacant apartments or houses were not advertised in the newspapers at all. Unspoken but obvious "steering" to specific neighborhoods was common. The Cincinnati Metropolitan Housing Authority could no longer legally separate public housing projects by race.

The nonprofit Better Housing League of Greater Cincinnati, a United Way agency, provided professional housing counseling for first-time and nontraditional homebuyers, but housing discrimination against low-income whites and minorities of all income levels continued throughout the century. Free legal advice to those who faced discrimination when seeking housing or applying for home mortgages was needed despite the 1964 Civil Rights Act.

Marian:

I became a founding member of Housing Opportunities Made Equal, HOME, in 1969.[21] I'm still a board member. You know, it is great fun to work with good people over so many years. We started out with a lot of volunteers, most of whom were "checkers," but volunteers worked in the office, too. Our agency directors, only three in forty-five years, and several staff members have always been very smart lawyers. If a black couple or family were told that the apartment or house they wanted to see had already been rented and it continued to be advertised, or if a landlord would accept only an application for rental from a black couple but would immediately rent to a white couple, we would act. We decided the only way to change these widespread practices was to gather the facts and file lawsuits under new federal fair-housing laws. We won many such suits until landlords learned they could not continue to discriminate.

We still need HOME, only now there are more complaints against landlords who won't allow children or rent to Hispanic families. I think the discrimination against blacks or mixed-race couples is a lot better than it used to be, but it's still out there even though it's against the law.

REPRODUCTIVE RIGHTS

Cincinnati has had historic support for family planning and early child health care. The nonprofit Babies' Milk Fund was established in 1909. There were public baby clinics in Mt. Auburn, Norwood, and Harrison, Ohio. The 1926 charter included a City Health Department with healthcare clinics for lower-income families throughout the city. There was strong financial support from local wealthy families and doctors in these early efforts.

Dr. Elizabeth Campbell, a physician, had a beautiful home and a medical practice in Mt. Auburn, close to the Christ Hospital. She willed her home to the Planned Parenthood Association of Cincinnati for use as a medical clinic for women.[22] A woman's right to comprehensive reproductive healthcare, including abortions, was strictly limited by law until 1973.

Cincinnati, with large Catholic and fundamentalist Christian populations, quickly developed a strong, organized Right-to-Life anti-abortion movement after the 1973 *Roe v. Wade* Supreme Court decision that legalized abortion. Planned Parenthood opened the Margaret Sanger Center specifically to provide abortion services in Mt. Auburn. The local Right-to-Life and several conservative churches began daily picketing of the Sanger Women's Health Care Center that continues today.

Beginning in 1978, there was a wave of physician assassinations, clinic bombings, arson attacks, and anthrax scares attempting to stop abortion services throughout the country.[23] Cincinnati did not escape the violence.

Approximately one hundred members of a group called Americans Against Abortion demonstrated in front of the local Sanger clinic in late 1985.[24] They held a mock funeral and exchanged words with about fifty members of the Freedom of Choice Coalition. Police watched but made no arrests. Shortly thereafter, fires were set at the Sanger Center and the nearby Women's Health Care Center about a mile away. Dr. Martin Haskell, director of the Women's Center, said the damage at his facility was confined mostly to the basement, but there was smoke damage throughout the building. When asked by a reporter if he thought the fires were linked, he said, "That's a logical assumption. We're not the first healthcare center to be firebombed."[25]

The Sanger Center had to suspend operations for six months until another temporary location could be found. In February 1987, a self-appointed member of the Army of God placed a pipe bomb outside the temporary offices of the Sanger Center. Fortunately, it was discovered and removed before it exploded.[26] John Brockhoeft, who later confessed and served seven years in prison for the local clinic fires, was successful at firebombing the recently repaired Sanger Center, causing $250,000 in damage. Dr. Campbell's former home and clinic had to be demolished and a new medical clinic built on the site. The attacks backfired to a large degree. Thousands of outraged citizens donated money to what is now Planned Parenthood of Southwest Ohio and a local Planned Parenthood Foundation was established. Marian became president of the foundation until 2012 and continues to serve on the Planned Parenthood Board of Trustees.

Marian's story:

My first exposure to the need for reproductive healthcare came when I was a child. We knew of a young girl in Gallipolis who died from a self-induced abortion at age fourteen. My mother explained what happened to Mildred and me. She said the girl should not have died: there should be adequate care for anybody in that girl's position. When I learned that Planned Parenthood had a strong emphasis on education for boys and girls, I began to actively support their clinics and education program. I gave them financial support for some years, but then I got directly involved as a volunteer Sanger Center patient escort, board member, and fundraiser.

The Right-to-Life people picketed the Margaret Sanger Center every day; they still do. They hold up horrible signs and have demonstrations that are uncivil. One of my friends said I taught her how to hold up her head and be an escort through those lines of people jeering and shouting at women coming into or out of the Sanger Center. It is terrible that women making difficult decisions have to run a gauntlet of opponents trying to block the way to the door of the clinic. It was important work. After the bombing and loss of the Campbell house, we established a Planned Parenthood Foundation. I was president of that until 2012 and I am still on the agency's board of trustees.

VOTING RIGHTS

Marian and Donald Spencer were plaintiffs in still another lawsuit in 2004. Ohio Attorney General Kenneth Blackwell, Marian's old city council colleague, proposed to challenge the registration of black voters in their polling places.

Marian:

There was another fight in 2004, about voting rights. Ken Blackwell, who is black but a conservative Republican, at least for now, wanted to place Republican voter challengers in African American precincts on Election Day. It was wrong.

Donald and I decided to seek a judicial temporary restraining order to stop what was clearly an attempt to intimidate black voters.[27] The suit was before Judge Susan Dlott, United States District Court, Southern District of Ohio. Our attorney was Alphonse Gerhardstein, a respected civil rights lawyer. The court hearing was held early in the evening.

Mr. Gerhardstein began questioning Marian about her history and asking her to describe situations where African Americans were treated differently than whites in any efforts to seek access to government services or public accommodations.

From the court record:[28]

A. I could cite so many, Mr. Gerhardstein, that there is an uncertainty, in my opinion, in the individual and the family life of black Americans, and there's an unease in the lives of all of us. It's the one true certainty I can assert. . . . Examples: The KKK march through the streets of Galllipolis, Ohio, my home. Ten years ago, I saw the Ku Klux Klan without hoods—they had hoods the first time—march without hoods in Gallipolis again, and in Angola, Indiana. Those are the recent times. . . . I can tell you of experiences of travel. I have been in restaurants and been questioned. When I was president of Quadres [at the University of Cincinnati], I had to take the faculty adviser, Malcolm MacGregor, who was a classics professor who knew nothing of discrimination, with me to see why the senior prom had to be held in a facility where all the students might attend without discrimination, without embarrassment. For the first time in its history, the university did not hold a prom. That was in 1942. We were told it was because of the war. But the real reason was because they did not want to fight the battle of opening downtown hotels.

I worked with Coney Island, as you have read in the newspaper. . . . All my life I have fought this kind of thing. I have fought it for my family; I have fought it for children, any place constituted in these United States. I have fought for justice because I believe in a functioning democracy. I think that access to the polling booth is extremely important to have a functioning democracy.

Q. Why did you bring the [Coney Island] case?

A. I brought this case because I thought our children should come up as equals in any part of our country. They should not feel that they were any different.

Q. What is it about the Republican deployment of the challengers in the African American precincts that causes you to come to federal court and seek relief?

A. Because you already have the challenging process there inside the voting booth. The thing that makes me think that this particular challenge is extraordinary, it seems to me to be overkill. I don't think it's necessary to have that many people inside a polling booth questioning people, having them line up, have less access.

I know I have voted since the redistricting two years ago. Many people went to the wrong polling place. The provisional balloting, I thought, if it allowed you to vote anyway, then it made sense. But when I read in the newspaper that [Attorney General] Kenneth Blackwell was changing that balloting, I thought this is wrong. This is wrong. We are voting too few in our country today to make our democracy work as well as it should. . . .

We have been able to have access without long lines keeping us from getting in. People who work late could come and get in before the polls closed. I've always been an unpaid poll worker on the outside from 6:30 a.m. to 7:30 at night, and I feel that it's a privilege. I would like to see everybody have the same privilege that gives them access without fear. I think this is discriminatory.

Q. What is it about the deployment of the Republican challengers that makes you concerned that African Americans will experience fear or intimidation?

A. As I've listened, I feel that the deployment is discriminatory in and of itself. If the black polling places are being presented with a large group of people from the outside to staff those polling places, they are not able to feel comfortable with them. I think it's overkill.

Q. And in your experience dealing with attempts to get access to government services, places of public accommodation, what do you expect will be the reaction of African Americans as they witness the interrogation of voters by precinct judges being prompted by the Republican challengers?

A. [Objection overruled] I think they would resent it. I go to the polling place in my neighborhood. I know the people in the booth, in the polling place. I know them as neighbors. I know them as people who expect you to be there. But they are not expecting you to be illegal as a voter. They are expecting you to come because you revel in the opportunity to cast a vote in a free society and not be challenged or overly harassed.

Q. If they are interrogated at the request of challengers, what will you expect the reaction of those in line behind and those in the room to be?

A. Well, the line behind are going to be upset because they're having to be held up—that they might be denied a vote because they can't stay. I'm wondering, too, about the new voter who is for the first time attempting to exercise his franchise, his or her franchise, and is wondering, Why am I being singled out?

Q. How does this ultimately make you feel when you look at your history of trying to integrate access to government services and accommodations and then you're here in federal court today in 2004?

A. I'm just grateful that I can be here and speak out, and I will continue to do so. In fact, I hope to live to be a hundred. I will still be speaking out every opportunity for equality and justice and access to the polling place.[29]

The temporary restraining order (TRO) was granted. It was immediately appealed by the Ohio Attorney General's office, that same evening.

The TRO was stayed by the court of appeals by 9:00 p.m., stopping the original order. Mr. Gerhardstein then appealed to the U.S. Supreme Court later that same night. The Supreme Court refused to hear the case, which meant the Spencers lost their case. However, the national news media had picked up the story of the suit and the dramatic appeals. This caused so much negative national publicity for the State of Ohio and the attorney general that Mr. Blackwell dropped the entire plan to place challengers in black voting precincts.[30] Marian said, "Well, we lost the battle but seemed to win that war, at least for a time."

National challenges to voting access continue and have increased. In 2014, the Hamilton County Board of Elections proposed moving their offices from downtown Cincinnati to suburban Mt. Airy, where there is limited public transportation for access to voter registration and early voting. Ohio now requires a government identification card with a photo to vote, both policies protested by Marian at public meetings. Marian continues to participate in the election process. Every election year, including 2014, she has always distributed up to two thousand copies of the League of Women Voter's *Who and What of Elections* to many local African American churches.

NATIONAL UNDERGROUND RAILROAD FREEDOM CENTER

In 2004, the National Underground Railroad Freedom Center opened in downtown Cincinnati on the banks of the Ohio River. Well known as the home of Harriet Beecher Stowe, the author of *Uncle Tom's Cabin*, Cincinnati was a major escape route for American slaves fleeing to Canada. The decade of planning and fundraising for, and building of, the National Underground Railroad Freedom Center included the appointment of Marian as an honorary cochair in 1998. Marian has said many times, "This country's history of slavery, the quest for freedom and equality, and the right to vote is vital to our democracy." Always with a smile and enthusiasm, she reminds museum visitors that this museum is not only about the remarkable history of the Underground Railroad, it pays tribute, hosts conferences, and provides education about all aspects of human enslavement. She remains a member of the museum's board of trustees.

Turning over leadership to another generation is a challenge to everyone. Marian, at ninety-five, has decided she should commit to no more than two meetings in a single day, and that her role is to serve primarily as historian and adviser.

Marian joined five past presidents of the local NAACP chapter in a significant challenge to the local leadership in 2013. The mismanagement charges were dismissed by the national NAACP office in March 2014 after election of a new local president and vice president.[31] That year, 2014, the Charter Committee of Cincinnati, which Marian has nurtured and supported for seventy-four years, began undergoing a major transformation with a new, energetic leadership taking on needed City Charter updates and reforms. Many issues, including the future role of the Charter Committee, are open to question. Marian is the on-site historian who occasionally reminds "these young Turks" of Charter's history before they were born.

Years may have passed, but the Alexander twins remain as close as ever. Marian and Mildred each received a personal letter from First Lady Michelle Obama in March 2014, thanking them for remembering Mrs. Obama's birthday and hoping she would have a chance to see them. Mildred has known Mrs. Obama for many years. In May, Marian and her son Edward visited Mildred in Maryland to see Mildred's new home.

That summer again found Marian at her beloved Fox Lake. Her Fox Lake friends and her family are always concerned about her 350-mile drive and arrival there. That year, for the first time, everyone insisted that Marian wear a life jacket when swimming in the lake. At midsummer, she reported by phone that she had not swum much—it was too cold—and the gifted life jacket was still in the back seat of her car. In September, a cousin traveled to Fox Lake to assist Marian in preparing the Fox Lake house for the winter and to help her drive home to Cincinnati.

Then, in November, Marian's resilience was again tested. Marian shopped at a Kroger grocery store near her home two days before Thanksgiving. Mildred was arriving by train from Washington, D.C., that day for the holiday. Members of the extended family planned to go to a restaurant for Thanksgiving dinner, but there would be many visitors in the coming days. The *Cincinnati Herald* weekly newspaper front-page headline and picture described what happened that day: "Feisty Marian Spencer, 94, runs to catch a thief."[32]

Marian had finished shopping and loading her groceries into her car. As the parking lot was quite full, she had parked at the edge of the lot, near a busy cross street. Once in her car, she placed her purse on the passenger seat and prepared to start the ignition, leaving her car window rolled down to let in fresh air. A young man, wearing a hooded sweatshirt that covered most of his face, reached into the window and put a gun to Marian's head. Anyone who saw him, Marian later said, would have thought he was just stopping to chat, which was a common occurrence. He quietly said, "Give me your pocketbook or I will kill you." Marian could not believe he would threaten to kill her. The robber then reached across Marian, snatched the purse out of her hand, and ran.

"I was so mad I just ran after him. How dare he! If he had asked for money I would have given him some. He must have needed it, but I was mad." As she chased the robber, Marian shouted that the man had stolen her purse. A bystander joined her, but the thief rounded an apartment building on the next corner and got away. "He was faster than me, but I am ninety-four," she said. The grocery store staff were kind and helpful; she waited in the employee break room until the police arrived. Marian had been to the bank and visited her lawyer that morning; she lost her house keys, wallet, insurance papers, and about one hundred dollars. She did not lose her nerve.

The good news that day was, when she returned home after filing a crime report, Mildred was there. Her sister had been picked up at the train station by her grandson. It was a relief to have Mildred with her in the house as all the locks had to be changed immediately and her stolen credit cards and checkbook reported. And, Marian had help answering the constant phone calls. The incident had not gone unnoticed. Articles and interviews from the *Cincinnati Enquirer*, two local television stations, and one radio station, and a personal apology from the retired president of the Kroger Company, David Dillon, ensued.

Mildred's visit and the family coming together for the holiday was a good distraction so Marian didn't have to think about being robbed. On Thanksgiving Day morning, Mildred's grandson arrived at the house with everything needed to cook dinner, which he did, and Marian hosted ten guests to celebrate her safety and their being together.

Marian's influence remains strong. Her voice and wisdom are sought throughout the community by leaders of every race and religion. Her general good cheer and enthusiasm for whatever she is doing continues. Wherever she is, Marian lights up the room. She also continues to swim at least once a week.

Later thoughts from Marian about recording her story:

There are so many more stories I could tell. So many issues keep coming back again and again, sometimes it's two steps forward and one step back, like this ongoing fight about voting rights. This country has fought over voting rights for 150 years! We need far more voters; we should consider how other countries get a good voter turnout. I think the white leadership should reconsider proportional representation in Cincinnati. They may need it when they become the minority group in the not too distant future.

People need to recognize that diversity is much more than just including blacks and whites. We need to have inclusion of all races, religions, and lifestyles working together for equality.

President Obama has helped us be more aware of our history— where we're going and where the next generation should be. We need to remember and consider our forward progress and work to make our democracy a true one. Every minority must recognize they are Americans: they have a stake in making our country all that it can and should be.

We've got to go forward. It is unbelievable that true Americans would even consider going back. Our biggest challenge for the future is inclusion of all people with equal status. You can't have some slave and some free. We need unanimity of philosophy around what it truly means to be an American. It is feasible this can be reached: we've got what it takes and the talent; we need people from all walks of life. We must never go back.

I am very hopeful for the future. We are facing some difficult times. Our immediate future is filled with contradictions. I believe the strongest, more positive, most thoughtful people will win and continue to make this country great.

Photographs

1955–present

Donald and Marian celebrate their fiftieth wedding anniversary with Mildred;
August 12, 1990

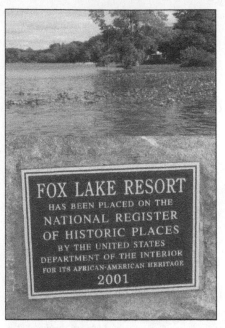

Fox Lake, an African American resort developed in 1927

In 1963 the Spencers built a summer home at Fox Lake

A caricature of Marian appeared in the *Cincinnati Post & Times Star*, November 21, 1972. *Photo courtesy of E. W. Scripps*

Mayor Theodore M. Berry with Marian during the campaign to preserve the proportional representation voting system, 1975

Marian and Donald, NAACP Life Members, 1982

Donald and Marian with their grandsons Oliver *(left)* and Matthew *(front)*, 1987

Marian with her men: grandson Oliver, Donald Jr., Donald Sr., and grandson Matthew

Cincinnati City Council members Bobbie Sterne and Marian Spencer, 1983

Cincinnati city officials pose at the riverfront groundbreaking, 1984: *(left to right)* Mayor Arnold Bortz and council members Kenneth Blackwell, Bobbie Sterne, and Marian

Vice Mayor Marian Spencer at Fountain Square, 1984

City Councilman Tom Brush, NAACP president Melvin Jones, Wendell Young, Marian, and Secretary of State Sherrod Brown during the 1985 city council campaign

Marian listens to city council election results at a local radio station, 1985

Marian, Senator John Glenn, and national NOW president Shirley Rosser, 1989

Donald and Marian Spencer with Cincinnati mayor Roxanne Qualls, 1993.
Photo courtesy of Brewster Rhoads

Ohio University Board of Trustees reception, 2007. Marian and Donald stand toward the right of the group.

University of Cincinnati president Nancy Zimpher at the Spencers' home for Donald's ninety-first birthday

Donald and Marian Spencer with Senator Barack Obama, 2008

Donald and Marian Spencer with Governor Ted Strickland, 2008

Donald and Marian Spencer with Michelle Obama, 2008

Edward, Priscilla, Donald Jr., Marian, and Donald Sr. celebrate Christmas, 2009

The extended Spencer family at Donald Sr.'s memorial service, May 14, 2010.
Photo courtesy of Brewster Rhoads

Great-grandson Emmanuel Brockman, 2012

Former mayor Bobbie Sterne and former vice mayor Marian Spencer.
Photo courtesy of Brewster Rhoads

Mildred Alexander Malcolm and Marian Alexander Spencer at age ninety-four, November 2014. *Photo courtesy of Barbara Wolf*

APPENDIX A

Family Tree

Marian and her twin sister Mildred at age ninety,
May 14, 2010. *Photograph courtesy of Brewster Rhoads*

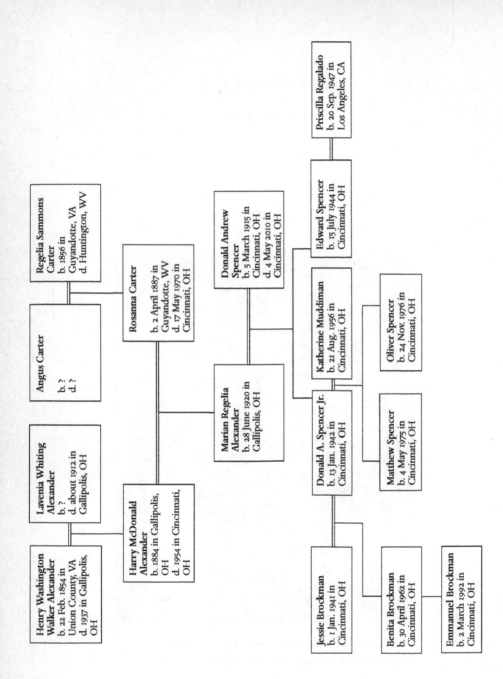

APPENDIX B

Awards

1968   National Conference of Christians and Jews; Certificate of Recognition

1972   Cincinnati Enquirer Woman of the Year Award

PUSH (People United to Save Humanity, Inc.) for Excellence Award

1980   NAACP President's Award for outstanding leadership

United States Commission on Civil Rights, two-year appointment

1982   Cincinnati Human Relations Commission; Ethelrie Harper Award

University of Cincinnati Department of Women's Studies Distinguished Alumna Award

YMCA Black Achievers Award

1983   Omega Psi Phi Fraternity and Mt. Auburn Community Council, "Black and Proud" Award

1984   YWCA Career Woman of Achievement

1985   Ohio Black Leadership Women's Award for outstanding performance

Black Career Women, Inc., Certificate of Appreciation

1986   National Association of Social Workers; Public Citizen of the Year

1987   Baptist Ministers Conference; Life Dedicated to Fulfillment of the Dream Award

1992   A. Philip Randolph Community Activist Award

Kentucky Colonel Inductee

Ohio Attorney General, Certificate of recognition for tireless efforts in defending civil rights and human rights

1993 Jacob E. Davis Volunteer Leadership Award

United Way; Joseph A. Hall Award for Promoting Diversity

1994 Center for Voting and Democracy; Third Annual Champion of Democracy Award

Ohio University Honorary Alumna Award

Urban League Heritage Award

1996 Long Distance Runner Award, for dedicated service to improve the lives of many

1997 Applause! Magazine Imagemaker Award

Housing Opportunities Made Equal (HOME); Founders Award

1998 Alpha Kappa Alpha Sorority; Golden Soror of the Year Award

Chamber of Commerce; Great Living Cincinnatians Award

National Underground Railroad Freedom Center; Gandhi, King, Ikeda Award for exemplary leadership for human rights and peace

1999 City of Cincinnati World of Appreciation Award

Alpha Kappa Alpha Sorority, Inc., Sigma Omega Chapter Diamond Soror Award

2001 Cincinnati Society of Association Executives, Statesman Award for distinguished deeds and notable achievements

Faith Community of St. Mark Catholic Church First Annual Dr. Martin Luther King Jr. "Keep the Dream Alive" Award

2002 Greater Cincinnati Community Shares, Maurice McCrackin Peace & Justice Special Recognition Award

2003 University of Cincinnati McMicken College Distinguished Alumni Award

Zeta Phi Beta Sorority, Inc. Beta Zeta Zeta Chapter, Lifetime Achievement Award

2006 University of Cincinnati Honorary Doctorate of Humane Letters

2007	Ohio University Honorary Doctorate of Letters
	Midwest Regional Black Family Reunion Celebration, Family of the Year Award to Donald and Marian Spencer
2008	Fifth Third Bank, WCPO-TV; Profiles in Courage Award
	University of Cincinnati Department of Women's Studies Outstanding Service Award
	Cincinnatus Association Honorary Membership
2009	Freedom Heritage Foundation of Columbus, Ohio; Humanitarian Award
2010	Ohio Civil Rights Commission, Ohio Civil Rights Hall of Fame
	Woman's City Club of Greater Cincinnati; Feisty Woman Award
	City of Cincinnati, June 28, 2010, "Marian Spencer Day" in Cincinnati
2011	YWCA Racial Justice Award
2012	Cincinnati City Council Proclamation for distinguished contributions by African Americans
	Cincinnati Women's Alliance; Jewel of the Community Award
	Marian Spencer Diversity Ambassador Award; created by the University of Cincinnati President's Diversity Council
	Ohio Realtist Association; Horace Sudduth Humanitarian Award for outstanding service and philanthropy
	Top Ladies of Distinction, Inc., Cincinnati chapter; Sweetheart Award, created for Marian Spencer
2013	Charter Committee of Greater Cincinnati, Charterite of the Year
	City of Cincinnati, June 2, 2013, "Marian Spencer Day" in Cincinnati
	Ohio State Senate, June 2, 2013, Exemplary Attainment proclamation
	National Underground Railroad Freedom Center; Dada Rafiki Sisters of Legacy Award

2014   Horizon Science Academy of Cincinnati; Golden Angel
        Freedom Fighter Award, recognized for outstanding
        accomplishments in bringing racial equality to Cincinnati in
        the area of public accommodations, fair housing and equality
        for women

        Sigma Omega Chapter; Alpha Kappa Alpha Sorority Salute,
        "Simply the Best" to Soror Marian Spencer on the Chapter's
        Ninetieth Anniversary

        Sigma Phi; Women's Honorary Tap Class for significant
        contributions toward creating better futures for women as a
        student and alumna of the University of Cincinnati

2015   Cincinnati State College Honorary Doctorate

APPENDIX C

Organizations: Memberships and Boards

American Civil Liberties Union
1933	Member
1984	Life member

Avondale Community Council
1952–present	Member

Center for Voting and Democracy
1990	Board of Trustees

Charter Committee of Cincinnati
1955–present	Board of Trustees

City of Cincinnati
1950	Mayor's Friendly Relations Committee
1973	Board of Education candidate
1983	First African American woman elected to city council
1983–1985	City Planning Commission
1984–1985	Vice Mayor

Common Cause
1970–present	Supporter

Fellowship House
1950–1965	Member
1953	President

Fox Lake Property Owners Association
2010–present	Board of Directors

Hoxworth Blood Center
1981–1987	Board of Trustees

Links, Inc., Cincinnati Chapter

1942–present	Life member
1942–1946	President

NAACP

1933	Member, joined as teenager in Gallipolis, OH
1952	Chair, Legal Defense Committee for Coney Island integration suit
1972	Chair, Education Committee for School Desegregation Suit
1980	First woman president of a local chapter
1982	Life member

National Underground Railroad Freedom Center

1998–present	Honorary cochair & board member

Ohio Civil Rights Commission

1980–1982	Member

Planned Parenthood Association of Southwest Ohio

1978–present	Board of Trustees
1980–2012	Foundation president

University of Cincinnati

1938–1942	Student
1938–1940	President of Quadres
1975–1979	Board of Trustees

Urban League of Greater Cincinnati

1944–present	Member
2010–present	Executive Committee, Board of Trustees

WCET Public Television

1987–1992	Board of Trustees

WGUC Public Radio

1982–1985	Board of Trustees

Woman's City Club

1952–present	Member
1971	First African American president

YWCA

1938–1942	President, Eighth Street/West End YW
1945	Vice president, Metropolitan YWCA
1948	Public Affairs Committee, instrumental in integrating YW housing, swimming pools, and summer camps nationally
	Board of Trustees

APPENDIX D

Marian Spencer Day Proclamation
June 28, 2010

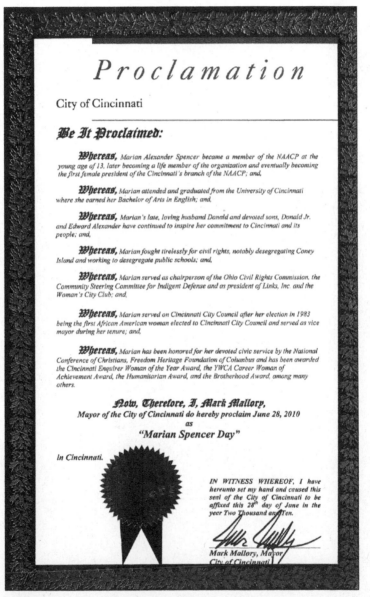

Proclamation

City of Cincinnati

Be It Proclaimed:

Whereas, Marian Alexander Spencer became a member of the NAACP at the young age of 13, later becoming a life member of the organization and eventually becoming the first female president of the Cincinnati's branch of the NAACP; and,

Whereas, Marian attended and graduated from the University of Cincinnati where she earned her Bachelor of Arts in English; and,

Whereas, Marian's late, loving husband Donald and devoted sons, Donald Jr. and Edward Alexander have continued to inspire her commitment to Cincinnati and its people; and,

Whereas, Marian fought tirelessly for civil rights, notably desegregating Coney Island and working to desegregate public schools; and,

Whereas, Marian served as chairperson of the Ohio Civil Rights Commission, the Community Steering Committee for Indigent Defense and as president of Links, Inc. and the Woman's City Club; and,

Whereas, Marian served on Cincinnati City Council after her election in 1983 being the first African American woman elected to Cincinnati City Council and served as vice mayor during her tenure; and,

Whereas, Marian has been honored for her devoted civic service by the National Conference of Christians, Freedom Heritage Foundation of Columbus and has been awarded the Cincinnati Enquirer Woman of the Year Award, the YWCA Career Woman of Achievement Award, the Humanitarian Award, and the Brotherhood Award, among many others.

Now, Therefore, I, Mark Mallory,
Mayor of the City of Cincinnati do hereby proclaim June 28, 2010
as
"Marian Spencer Day"

In Cincinnati.

IN WITNESS WHEREOF, I have hereunto set my hand and caused this seal of the City of Cincinnati to be affixed this 28th day of June in the year Two Thousand and Ten.

Mark Mallory, Mayor
City of Cincinnati

APPENDIX E

Marian Spencer Day Proclamation
June 2, 2013

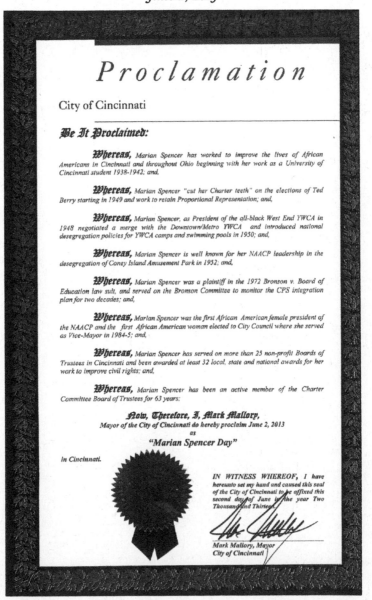

Proclamation

City of Cincinnati

Be It Proclaimed:

Whereas, Marian Spencer has worked to improve the lives of African Americans in Cincinnati and throughout Ohio beginning with her work as a University of Cincinnati student 1938-1942; and,

Whereas, Marian Spencer "cut her Charter teeth" on the elections of Ted Berry starting in 1949 and work to retain Proportional Representation; and,

Whereas, Marian Spencer, as President of the all-black West End YWCA in 1948 negotiated a merge with the Downtown/Metro YWCA and introduced national desegregation policies for YWCA camps and swimming pools in 1950; and,

Whereas, Marian Spencer is well known for her NAACP leadership in the desegregation of Coney Island Amusement Park in 1952; and,

Whereas, Marian Spencer was a plaintiff in the 1972 Bronson v. Board of Education law suit, and served on the Bronson Committee to monitor the CPS integration plan for two decades; and,

Whereas, Marian Spencer was the first African American female president of the NAACP and the first African American woman elected to City Council where she served as Vice-Mayor in 1984-5; and,

Whereas, Marian Spencer has served on more than 25 non-profit Boards of Trustees in Cincinnati and been awarded at least 32 local, state and national awards for her work to improve civil rights; and,

Whereas, Marian Spencer has been an active member of the Charter Committee Board of Trustees for 63 years;

Now, Therefore, I, Mark Mallory,
Mayor of the City of Cincinnati do hereby proclaim June 2, 2013
as
"Marian Spencer Day"

In Cincinnati.

IN WITNESS WHEREOF, I have hereunto set my hand and caused this seal of the City of Cincinnati to be affixed this second day of June in the year Two Thousand and Thirteen.

Mark Mallory, Mayor
City of Cincinnati

APPENDIX F

Ohio Senate Proclamation
June 2, 2013

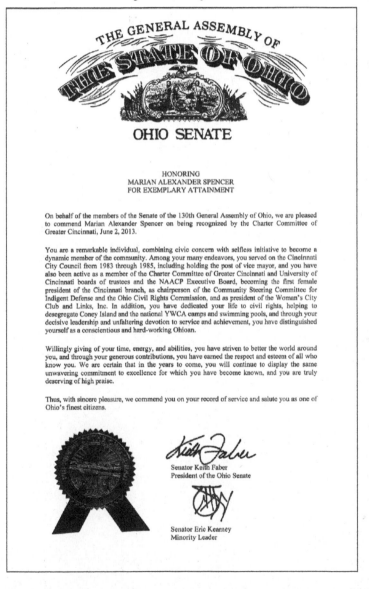

THE GENERAL ASSEMBLY OF
THE STATE OF OHIO

OHIO SENATE

HONORING
MARIAN ALEXANDER SPENCER
FOR EXEMPLARY ATTAINMENT

On behalf of the members of the Senate of the 130th General Assembly of Ohio, we are pleased to commend Marian Alexander Spencer on being recognized by the Charter Committee of Greater Cincinnati, June 2, 2013.

You are a remarkable individual, combining civic concern with selfless initiative to become a dynamic member of the community. Among your many endeavors, you served on the Cincinnati City Council from 1983 through 1985, including holding the post of vice mayor, and you have also been active as a member of the Charter Committee of Greater Cincinnati and University of Cincinnati boards of trustees and the NAACP Executive Board, becoming the first female president of the Cincinnati branch, as chairperson of the Community Steering Committee for Indigent Defense and the Ohio Civil Rights Commission, and as president of the Woman's City Club and Links, Inc. In addition, you have dedicated your life to civil rights, helping to desegregate Coney Island and the national YWCA camps and swimming pools, and through your decisive leadership and unfaltering devotion to service and achievement, you have distinguished yourself as a conscientious and hard-working Ohioan.

Willingly giving of your time, energy, and abilities, you have striven to better the world around you, and through your generous contributions, you have earned the respect and esteem of all who know you. We are certain that in the years to come, you will continue to display the same unwavering commitment to excellence for which you have become known, and you are truly deserving of high praise.

Thus, with sincere pleasure, we commend you on your record of service and salute you as one of Ohio's finest citizens.

Senator Keith Faber
President of the Ohio Senate

Senator Eric Kearney
Minority Leader

APPENDIX G

Ohio Senate Proclamation
Renaming Frederick Douglass School

THE GENERAL ASSEMBLY OF THE STATE OF OHIO

OHIO SENATE

HONORING
MARIAN SPENCER
FOR EXEMPLARY ACCOMPLISHMENT

On behalf of the members of the Senate of the 128th General Assembly of Ohio, we extend special recognition to Marian Spencer on the former Frederick Douglass School building being named in honor of you and your late husband, Donald A. Spencer.

In being selected for this noteworthy distinction, you have been recognized as a dynamic member of your community. The widow of the late Donald Spencer, you are a former member of the Cincinnati City Council, and you sued to desegregate Coney Island in 1952. You have expended countless hours and seemingly inexhaustible energy in the interest of others, and it is through the efforts and consistent support of individuals such as you that our state has remained responsive to the diverse needs of its residents.

A gifted individual, you have directed yourself toward numerous worthwhile endeavors and have set an example worthy of emulation. Over the years, you have gained the admiration of all who know you, and you can be justifiably proud of your recent accomplishment.

Thus, with genuine pride, we commend you on your invaluable contributions to the community and salute you as a fine Ohioan.

Senator Bill Harris
President of the Ohio Senate

Senator Eric Kearney
9th Senatorial District

APPENDIX H

Interview of James Campbell, age 86
Gallipolis, Ohio, 1938

Hallie Miller, Reporter
Audrey Meighen, Author-Editor

Slave Narratives, A Folk History of Slavery in the United States
The Federal Writer's Project 1936–1938
Ohio Narratives, Vol XII, pg 18–21
Works Progress Administration
Library of Congress
Washington D.C.

The following interview of Marian's Uncle Jim Campbell, in Gallipolis, Ohio, in 1938, recently came to Marian's attention. Until 2014, Marian had never known her great-grandmother's name, Dinnah, nor had she heard any stories about the Alexander plantation in Virginia. Neither Marian's Grandfather Henry nor his brother, Uncle Jim, who together came to Gallipolis, ever talked about their experience in slavery. Marian's major regret is that she did not ask them about life before Emancipation. Until Marian saw this interview, she did not know whether her family had suffered badly at the hands of their slave master. Uncle Jim identifies several siblings who may have been born after Emancipation. Marian does not know about them. It is striking that Marian's family, like other African American families, rose to prominence out of slavery within living memory.

"Well, I'se bo'n Monro' Couty, West Virginia, on January 18, 1852[1], jes' few miles from Union, West Virginia."

---

[1] James Campbell was the younger half brother of Henry Alexander. Henry's birthdate on his tombstone is 1854. The northwestern counties of the Commonwealth of Virginia seceded from Virginia and became West Virginia immediately after the election of President Abraham Lincoln in 1860.

"My mammy was Dinnah Alexander Campbell an' my pappy was Levi Campbell an' day bof cum from Monro' County. Dat's 'bout only place I heard dem speak 'bout."

"Der wus Levi, Floyd, Henry, Noah, an' Nancy, jes' my haf brudders an' sistah, but I neber knowed no difrunce but whut day wuz my sistahs an' brudders."

"Where we liv? On Marse[2] John Alexander's farm, he wuz a good Marse too. All Marse John want wuz plenty wurk dun and we dun it too, so der wuz no trubble on ouah plantashun. I neber reclec' anyone gittin' whipped or bad treatment frum him. I does 'member, dat sum de neighbers say day was treated prutty mean, but I don't 'member much 'bout it 'caise I'se leetle den."

"Wher'd I sleep? I neber fergit dat trun'l bed, dat I sleep in."

"Marse John's place kinda stock farm an' I dun de milkin'. You all know dat wuz easy like so I jes' kcep busy milkin' an' gits out de hard work. Nudder thing I lik to do wuz pick berries, dat wuz easy too, so I dun my shar' pickin'."

"Money? Lawsy chile, I neber dun seen any money 'til aftah I dun cum to Gallipolis aftah der war. An' how I lik' to hear it jingle, if I jes' had two cents, I'd make it jingle."

"We all had plenty an' good things to eat, beans, corn, tatahs, melons an' hot mush, corn bread; we jes' seen white flour wunce in a while."

"Yes mam, we had rabbit, wil' turkey, pheasunts, an' fish, say I'se telling' you-all dat riful pappy had shue cud kill de game."

"Nudder good ole time wuz maple sugar makin' time, mostly dun at night by limestone burnin'. Yes, I heped with the 'lasses an' all de time I wuz thinkin' 'bout dem hot biscets, ham meat, corn bread an' 'lasses."

"We liv in a cabin on Marse John's place. Der wuzn't much in de cabin but my mammy kept it mighty clean. Say, I kin see dat ole' fiah place wid de big logs a burnin' right now; uh, an' smell dat good cookin', all dun in iron pots an' skillets. An' all de cookin' an' heatin' wuz dun by wood, why I nebber seed a lump o' coal all time I wuz der. We all had to cut so much wood an' pile it up two weeks 'for Christmas, an' den when ouah pile wuz cut, den ouah wurk wuz dun, so we'd jes hav good time."

---

[2]Master

"We all woah jeans clos', jes pants an' jacket. In de summah we chilluns all went barefoot, but in de wintah we all woah shoes."

"Ol' Marse John an' his family live in a big fine brick hous'. Marse John had des chilluns, Miss Betty an' Miss Ann an' der wuz Marse Mike an' Marse John. Marse John, he wuz sorta spiled lik. He dun wen to de war an' runs 'way frum Harper's Ferry an' cum home jes' sceered to death. He get himsef a pah o' crutches an' nebr goes back. Marse John dun used dem crutches 'til aftah de war wuz ovah. Den der wuz ol' Missy Kimberton—de gran' muthah. She wuz 'culiar but prutty good, so wuz Marse's chilluns."

"Ol' Marse John had bout 20 slaves so de wurk wuzn't so bad on nun ob us. I kin jes' see dem ol' bindahs and harrows now, dat day used den. It would shure look funny usin' 'em now."

"I all'us got up foah clock in de mornin' to git in de cows an' I didn't hurry nun, 'caise dat tak in de time."

"Ouah mammy neber 'lowed de old folks to tell us chilluns sceery stories o' hants an' sich lik' so der's nun foah me to 'member."

"Travelin' wuz rather slo' lik. De only way wuz in ox-carts or on hoss back. We all didn't hav much time for travelin'. Our Marse wuz too good to think 'bout runnin' 'way."

"Nun my fam'ly cud read or write. I lurned to read an write aftah I cum Norf to Ohio. Dat wuz biggest thing I ebber tackled, but it made me de happies' aftah I learn't."

"We all went to Sunday School an' meetin'. Yes mam, we had to wurk on Sundays, too, if we did have any spare time, we went visitin'. On Saturday nights we had big time foah der wuz mos' all'us dancin' an' we'd dance long as de can'les lasted. Can'les wuz all we had any time fur light."

"I 'member one de neighbah boys tried to run 'way an' de patrollahs got 'im and' fetched 'im back an' he shure dun got a wallopin' for it. Dat dun tuk any sich notion out my head. Dem patrollahs dun keep us skeered to deaf all de time. One, Henry Jones, runned off and went cleah up Norf sum place an' day neber git im. 'Course we all wuz shure powahful glad 'bout his 'scapin'."

We'se neber 'lowed out de cabin at night. But sum times de oldah 'uns wud sneak out at night an' tak de hosses an' tak a leetle ride. An' man it wud bin jes' too bad if ol' Marse John ketched 'em: dat wuz shure heaps o' fun fer de kids. I 'member hearin' wunce de ol' folks talkin' 'bout de way one Marse dun sum black boys dat dun sumthin' wrong. He jes' make 'em bite off de heads o' baccer[3] wurms; mysef I'd ruther tuk a lickin."

"On Christmas Day, we'd git fish crackahs an' drink brandy, dat wuz all. Dat day wuz only one we did't wurk. On Saturday even's we'd mold can'les, dat wuzn't so bad."

"De happies' time o' my life wuz when Cap'n Tipton, a Yankee soljer cumd an' tol' us de wah wuz ober an' we wuz free. Cap'n Tipton sez, 'Youse de boys we dun dis foah.' We shure didn't lose no time gittin' 'way; no man."

"We went to Lewisburg an' den up to Cha'leston by wagon an' den tuk de guvment boat, Genrul Crooks, an' it brung us heah to Gallipolis in 1865. Dat Ohio shoah shure looked prutty."

"I'se shure thankful to Mr. Lincoln foah whut he dun foah us folks, but Jeff Davis, well I ain't sayin' whu I'm thinkin'."

" 'de is jes' like de worl', der is lots o' good an' lots o' bad in it."

---

[3]Tobacco worms

NOTES

Introduction

1. Cameron McWhirter, *Red Summer: The Summer of 1919 and the Awakening of Black America* (New York: MacMillan, 2011).

2. Nathan Irvin Huggins, *Harlem Renaissance* (New York: Oxford University Press, 2007); George Hutchinson, *The Harlem Renaissance in Black and White* (Cambridge, MA: Harvard University Press, 1995); Ellen Carol DuBois, *Woman Suffrage and Women's Rights* (New York: New York University Press, 1998).

3. Sara Evans, *Personal Politics: The Roots of Women's Liberation in the Civil Rights Movement and the New Left* (New York: Knopf Doubleday Publishing Group, 2010).

4. Victoria W. Wolcott, *Race, Riots, and Roller Coasters: The Struggle Over Segregated Recreation in America* (Philadelphia: University of Pennsylvania Press, 2012), 88–107.

5. Gina Ruffin Moore, *Cincinnati* (Charleston, SC: Arcadia Publishing, 2007), 31, 71–74; Kevin Grace, *Legendary Locals of Cincinnati, Ohio* (Charleston, SC: Arcadia Publishing, 2011), 119.

Chapter 1. A Remarkable Family in Twentieth-Century Gallipolis, Ohio

1. "Black History Rich in Gallia County," *Gallipolis (OH) Daily Tribune*, Feb. 2, 1987; William Wayne Griffin, *African Americans and the Color Line in Ohio, 1915–1930* (Columbus, OH: Ohio State University Press, 2005), 68–70.

2. Isabel Wilkerson, *The Warmth of Other Suns: The Epic Story of America's Great Migration* (New York: Vintage Books, 2011), 8–9.

3. Donald A. Spencer (husband of Marian Spencer), in discussion with author, 2000.

4. "Location and Population," City of Gallipolis, last modified 2012, http://www.cityofgallipolis.com/commissioners/population_and_location.php (accessed

September 1, 2014). Ohio History Central, http://www.ohiohistorycentral .org/w/Gallipolis,_Ohio (accessed February 25, 2015). "Population for Ohio Cities 1900–2000," Cleveland State University, http://www.urban.csuohio.edu/nodis/ historic/pop_place19002000.pdf.

5. "Cabell County History," Cabell County, West Virginia, last modified August 1, 2000, http://www.cabellcounty.org/History/history.htm (accessed August 14, 2014).

6. Eric Foner, *Reconstruction: America's Unfinished Revolution, 1863–1877* (New York: Harper and Row, 1988), 354–55.

7. Henry Alexander Wise IV (descendant of Governor Wise and Leslie Edwards, great-grandson of William Henry Grey), in discussion with author, October 27, 2005; Republic National Convention, *Presidential Election, 1872. Proceedings of the National union Republican Convention held at Philadelphia, June 5 and 6, 1872 . . . Reported by Francis H. Smith, Official reporter,* (Washington, D.C.: Gibson Brothers, 1872), 19.

8. Foner, *Reconstruction*, 26.

9. Ibid., 582.

10. Kurt R. Bell, "Tears, Trains and Triumphs: The Historical Legacy of African Americans and Pennsylvania's Railroads," *Milepost*, (September 1998); James W. Loewen, *Sundown Towns: A Hidden Dimension of American Racism* (New York: Touchstone, 2005), 43.

11. Loewen, *Sundown Towns*, 41.

12. Ibid., 197.

13. Frank U. Quillen, *The Color Line in Ohio: History of Race Prejudice in a Typical Northern State* (Ann Arbor, MI: G. Wahr, 1913); McWhirter, *Red Summer*.

14. Loewen, *Sundown Towns*, 4, 9. Anna, Illinois, was said to stand for "Ain't No Niggers After Dark." "Nigger Read This Sign and Run" was posted in Sunman, Indiana; Wallace, Iowa; and Manitowoc, Wisconsin; among other places. "NIGGER, Don't Let the Sun Set on You In Our Town" was the norm in Indiana, Illinois, Oklahoma, Iowa, and Idaho; it was still posted in Hawthorne, California, as late as 1960.

15. "West Virginia Water Laws, Water Regulations, and Water Rights," West Virginia Department of Environmental Protection, http://www.dep/wv/gov /WWE/wateruse/Documents/WV_WaterLaws.pdf (accessed August 31, 2014). The bridge was under West Virginia jurisdiction.

16. Henrietta C. Evans, John E. Lester, and Mary P. Wood. *Gallipolis, Ohio, Gallia County: A Pictorial History, 1790–1990* (Charleston, WV: Pictorial Histories Publishing Co., 1990), 92.

17. James Sands, "Stories of Success from Lincoln School Students," *Gallipolis (OH) Daily Tribune*, February 16, 1997.

18. Ronald E. Mickens, "Edward A. Bouchet: The First Black Ph.D.," *Black Collegian* 8, no. 4 (March/April 1978): 32; "Edward A. Bouchet, Ph.D.," *Negro History Bulletin* 31 (December 1968): 11.

19. *Manual of the Public Schools of Gallipolis and Course of Studies & Regulations of the Washington Academy High School and Lincoln High School*, (Gallipolis, OH, September 1900).

20. John Cross, "Whispering Pines: A Key to Success," last modified April 25, 2011, http://www.bowdoindailysun.com/2011/04/whispering-pines-a-key-to-success/ (accessed August 14, 2014). No copy of the address is available.

21. James Sands, "Hunger for Education Common Among Early Blacks," *Gallipolis (OH) Sunday Times-Sentinel*, February 28, 1993, A7.

22 *Brown v. Board of Education of Topeka*, 347 U.S. 483 (1954), landmark United States Supreme Court case in which the Court declared state laws establishing separate public schools for black and white students unconstitutional, http://www.law.cornell.edu/supremecourt/text/347/483.

23. "Girl Twins Make Remarkable Record in Ohio School," *Pittsburgh Courier*, April 16, 1938.

24. Nina Rastogi, "Who's the Heroine of *The Help?*," last modified August 9, 2011, http://www.slate.com/blogs/browbeat/2011/08/09/the_help_kathryn_stockett_s_novel_gets_made_into_a_movie.html (accessed September 2, 2014). *The Help* refers to the 2009 novel by Kathryn Stockett and the movie based on the book released in 2011.

25. "Guyandotte Civil War Days, Thunder in the Village," last modified 2009. http://www.guyandottecivilwardays.com/ (accessed August 14, 2014).

26. Larry Sonis, "Cabell County," e-WV: The West Virginia Encyclopedia, http://www.wvencyclopedia.org/articles/792 (last modified May 31, 2013, accessed on August 14, 2014).

27. Yvonne Brown, a first cousin who grew up in Grannie's house, said the story was told often by Grannie.

28. "Community of Guyandotte full of rich history," *Herald Dispatch* (Huntington, WV), June 28, 2010, http://www.herald-dispatch.com/news/x1093607941/Community-of-Guyandotte-full-of-rich-history. Family legend has it that this was General Sherman, known for his slash-and-burn tactics. It was, however, Colonel John L. Ziegler, who led the West Virginia Volunteers to recapture the town.

29. "Gallia County Emancipation Committee Nomination for 2014," *Gallia Hometown Herald* (Gallia County, OH), April 25, 2014, http://www.galliaherald.com/blog/2014/04/25/gallia-county-emancipation-committee-nomination-for-2014/. This former church is now the John Gee Black Historical Center. The center formerly hosted the only continuous Emancipation Day celebration in the country (since 1883). The celebration is now held at the Gallia County Fairgrounds.

1. John Kiesewetter, "Civil unrest woven into city's history," *Cincinnati Enquirer,* July 15, 2001, http://www.enquirer.com/editions/2001/07/15/tem_civil_unrest_woven.html.

2. Pulitzer Prize winner and Cincinnati native Jim Borgman has published countless political cartoons depicting this divide between East and West. Many of those images are accessible at http://www.borgman.cincinnati.com under the tab "Archive."

3. Dick Perry, *Vas You Ever In Zinzinnati? A Personal Portrait of Cincinnati* (New York: Weathervane Books, 1966), 110.

4. Iola Hessler Silberstein, *Cincinnati, Then and Now* (Cincinnati, OH: Voters Service Education Fund of the League of Women Voters of the Cincinnati Area, 1982), 283.

5. Writers' Program of the Work Projects Administration in the State of Ohio, *Cincinnati: A Guide to the Queen City and Its Neighbors* (Cincinnati, OH: Wiesen-Hart Press, 1943), 253–54.

6. Geoff Williams, "Local Life and Lore in Cincinnati," HGTV, http://www.frontdoor.com/places/local-life-and-lore-in-cincinnati (accessed September 5, 2014); Joan Fox, "A Rarefied View from the East Side. Snobby? You betcha," and Stephen Koff, "A Hot Retort from the West. Defensive? You betcha." *Cincinnati Magazine* (July 1985) 40–45.

7. Silberstein, *Cincinnati,* 215. Works Progress Administration was one of many federal job programs following the Great Depression.

8. Reginald C. McGrane, *The University of Cincinnati: A Success Story in Urban Higher Education* (New York: Harper and Row, 1963), 294.

9. Ibid., 294.

10. Silberstein, *Cincinnati,* 279.

11. Ibid., 240.

12. Ibid., 202.

13. Ibid., 229.

14. Rachel E. Powell, *Lighting the Fire, Leading the Way: The Woman's City Club of Greater Cincinnati 1965–2015,* (Cincinnati, OH: Woman's City Club of Greater Cincinnati, Inc., March 2015) Appendix I Timeline.

15. Enid Ginsberg (a concert participant), conversation with author, May 25, 2014.

16. Perry, *Vas you Ever,* 108.

17. Marian Spencer, interview with author, May 14, 2012.

18 . Deborah Rieselman, "African American Heritage at UC," *UC Magazine*, last modified May 2000, http://www.magazine.uc.edu/issues/0500/legends. html (accessed September 18, 2014).

19. McGrane, *University of Cincinnati*, 294.

20. Ibid., 293. McGrane reports a new sorority, Alpha Delta Pi, in 1935. The UC administration was concerned that allowing black organizations on campus would encourage them to organize in opposition to several campus policies.

21. Marian Spencer, interview, March 13, 2012.

22 "Dr. Donald A. Spencer In His Own Words: 'My life has been very full,'" *Cincinnati Herald*, May 8, 2010, B1. This piece was published posthumously.

23. Connie Springer, "Don Spencer: 'What Cha Doin' Now,' To Make A Better World" (unpublished article, 2008), in author's possession.

24. Robert B. Fairbanks, *Making Better Citizens: Housing Reform and the Community Development Strategy in Cincinnati, 1890–1960* (Urbana-Champaign, IL: University of Illinois Press, 1988), ch. 9. There had been a long, controversial fight over allowing blacks to live in the new public housing.

25. Charles P. Taft, *City Management: The Cincinnati Experience* (New York: Farrar and Rinehart, 1933). The Charter Committee is the oldest local independent political party in the country. Marian continues as a board member of the Charter Committee, http://www.chartercommittee.org.

26. The Links, Incorporated, *Links 60th Anniversary Report*, 2012. The Links, Incorporated, is an international not-for-profit corporation that consists of twelve-thousand professional women of color who are individual achievers and have made a difference in their communities and the world. The Cincinnati chapter had raised more than $1.2 million for educational programs and scholarships in the Greater Cincinnati area by 2012.

27. The Donald and Marian Spencer Giving Society, recognizing Urban League donors who have donated a total of $100,000, is named in honor of the Spencers.

28. Andrea Tuttle Kornbluh, *Lighting the Way: The Woman's City Club of Cincinnati, 1915–1965* (Cincinnati, OH: Young and Klein, 1986).

29. Spencie Love, *One Blood: The Death and Resurrection of Charles R. Drew* (Chapel Hill, NC: University of North Carolina Press, 1996). Drew, an African American, invented blood transfusions. A'Lelia Bundles, *On Her Own Ground: The Life and Times of Madam C. J. Walker* (New York: Scribner, 2002). Madame Walker was the first female African American millionaire. She developed hair lotion and products that addressed special characteristics of African Ameri-can women.

30. *Woman's City Club: Voices from 1965–2015*, Barbara Wolf, videographer (Cincinnati, OH: Woman's City Club of Greater Cincinnati, March 2015). "Dolls for

Democracy," *Missouri Times* (Columbia, MO: The State Historical Society of Missouri, May 2009), http://shs.umsystem.edu.

31. Mary Linn White, "I Hope I Never Feel There's Nothing to Do," *Cincinnati Post & Times Star*, November 21, 1972, 31.

Chapter 3. Family Life

1. After the death of Marian's father, Marian frequently called or referred to Donald Sr. as "Daddy."

2. Tom Lewis, *Divided Highways: Building the Interstate Highways, Transforming American Life* (Ithaca, NY: Cornell University, 2013).

3. Frank Rowsome Jr., *The Verse by the Side of the Road* (New York: E. P. Dutton and Co., 1965).

4. "The History of the Negro Motorist Green Books," Lerner Publishing, Inc., last modified 2010, http://www.bpl.org/general/associates/history_green_book.pdf (accessed September 2, 2014).

5. Loewen, *Sundown Towns*, 94. Some counties in Kansas and Missouri had a "Dead Line." Road signs at the county line simply said "No Negroes Allowed."

6. Ibid., 21; Millard F. Rogers Jr., *John Nolen and Mariemont: Building a New Town in Ohio* (Baltimore, MD: Johns Hopkins University Press, 2001); John Nolen, *New Towns for Old (1927): Achievements in Civic Improvement in Some American Small Towns and Neighborhoods* (Amherst, MA: University of Massachusetts Press, 2005).

7. Judith A. Blackburn and Robert M. Coughlin, *Building the Beloved Community: Maurice McCrackin's Life for Peace and Civil Rights* (Bloomington, IN: Trafford Publishing, 2006).

8. Emma Lou Thornbrough, *Indiana Blacks in the Twentieth Century* (Bloomington, IN: Indiana University Press, 2001); John Martin Smith, *Angola and Steuben County in Vintage Postcards* (Mount Pleasant, SC: Arcadia Publishing, 2001).

9. "African American History Month, 2002, Fox Lake: Angola, Indiana," National Register of Historic Places, last modified 2002, http://www.nps.gov/Nr/feature/afam/2002/foxlake.htm (accessed September 5, 2014).

10. "State and County Quick Facts: Norwood (city), Ohio," United States Census Bureau, http://www.quickfacts.census.gov/qfd/states/39/3957386.html (accessed September 5, 2014). Norwood, Ohio, a sundown town until the 1980s, is completely surrounded by the City of Cincinnati. The City of Norwood School District was initially included in the 1972 Bronson School Board segregation lawsuit. African Americans count as 7.6 percent of the Norwood population in 2010.

11. Nina Mijagkij, *Light in the Darkness: African Americans and the YMCA, 1852–1946* (Lexington, KY: University of Kentucky Press, 1994); Judith R. Blau, *Finessing Segregation, Integration, and Independence: The Atlanta's YMCAs, 1858–1993* (New Haven, CT: Yale University, 1994); Nancy Marie Robertson, *Christian Sisterhood, Race Relations, and the YWCA, 1906–1946* (Urbana-Champaign, IL: University of Illinois Press, 2007).

12. Walnut Hills High School boasts a top-rated, college-preparatory academic program regularly recognized in the top ten public high schools in the country.

13. Barbara Wolf, "Woman's City Club Centennial" video interview, November 11, 2013. Spencer states Jewish Hospital is there because Jewish and black physicians were barred from the other hospitals. Jewish Hospital was built in 1850. Jewish and Gentile physicians, including African Americans, were admitted to practice. Daniel J. Kenny, *Illustrated Cincinnati: A Pictorial Handbook of the Queen City* (Cincinnati, OH: Robert Clarke and Co., 1875), 49; Robert Katz, "Continuing Their Mission, Jewish Hospitals Reinvest in Philanthropy," last modified June 18, 2008, http://www.forward.com/articles/13591/continuing-their-mission-jewish-hospitals-reinves-/ (accessed September 5, 2014).

Chapter 4. Desegregation Suits and Continuing Battles

1. Coney Island, "History," http://www.coneyislandpark.com/history.php (accessed September 5, 2014).

2. Charles J. Jacques, *Cincinnati's Coney Island: America's Finest Amusement Park* (Jefferson, OH: Amusement Park Journal, 2002); Steve Kenne, "Getaway Became Coney Island," Cincinnati.com, last modified September 10, 2010, http://www.2.cincinnati.com/blogs/ourhistory/2010/09/20/getaway-became-coney-island (accessed September 5, 2014).

3. Walter P. Herz, *America's Civil War: Legacies in Cincinnati, Facilitators Training Manual for Public Forum* (Cincinnati, OH: Cincinnati Museum Center, October 27, 2005).

4. Nikki Taylor, *America's First Black Socialist: The Radical Life of Peter H. Clark* (Lexington, KY: University Press of Kentucky, 2013). For information on the Ohio Historical Marker at the site of Gaines High School, Cincinnati, Ohio, see Remarkable Ohio: Marking Ohio's History, "Marker #65-31 Gaines High School/Peter H. Clark," http://www.remarkableohio.org/HistoricalMarker.aspx?historicalMarkerId=1075 (accessed September 5, 2014).

5. Herz, *America's Civil War.*

6. Ibid.

7. Silberstein, *Cincinnati,* 93.

8. Ibid., 240.

9. Ibid., 244.

10. "Population Shifts Hamper Desegregation," *Cincinnati Post & Times Star,* June 19, 1971.

11. Silberstein, *Cincinnati,* 260.

12. ". . . Here Warned on Segregation," *Cincinnati Post & Times Star,* January 19, 1972; "Study Shows Percentage of Blacks in Cincinnati Schools," *Cincinnati Post & Times Star,* July 11, 1972.

13. Thomas A. Kessinger, "Legal Efforts Toward Desegregation of Education in Cincinnati," *American Educational History Journal* 32, no. 1 (Spring 2005): 89. *Tina Deal v. Board of Education,* 1963. On May 4, 1971, the U.S. Supreme Court dismissed the case. This upheld the U.S. District Court of Appeals ruling that the "Cincinnati school board was not guilty of practicing segregation and that it could not be held accountable for housing patterns which caused some schools to be segregated on the side of black or white."

14. "School Board Candidates Given OK To Discuss Desegregation Lawsuit," *Cincinnati Enquirer,* July 9, 1977, C2:3.

15. "Local Desegregation Suit Is Postponed Indefinitely," *Cincinnati Enquirer,* November 6, 1979, D1:5.

16. E. R. Shipp, "Cincinnati School Pact Is Embraced as a Model," *New York Times,* late edition, February 17, 1984, A16.

17. "Population Shifts Hamper Desegregation," *Cincinnati Post & Times Star.*

18. Sandy Buchanan, "History of Ohio Citizen Action's right-to-know campaigns," *Ohio Citizen Action* (February 1997), last modified September 18, 2014, http://www.ohiocitizen.org/campaigns/rtk/righttoknow.html (accessed September 18, 2014).

19. "Spencer's Study of Communities Called Political," *Cincinnati Enquirer,* September 18, 1985. F1:5.

20. Jim Borgman, editorial cartoon, *Cincinnati Enquirer,* November 10, 1985, D1.

21. Visit HOME's website at http://www.cincyfairhousing.com/.

22. Planned Parenthood of Southwest Ohio operates the Elizabeth Campbell Medical Center located at 2314 Auburn Avenue.

23. Melody Rose, *Abortion: A Documentary and Reference Guide,* (Santa Barbara, CA: ABC-CLIO, 2008), 206.

24. Mary McCarty and Michael Graham, "Abortion: Cincinnati's Civil War. How will it End?," *Cincinnati Magazine* (April 1990), 93–96.

25. United Press International, "Two Abortion Clinic Fires in Cincinnati, Blazes 1½ Miles Apart Follow 'Mock Funeral,'" *Chicago Tribune*, December 31, 1985, http://www.articles.chicagotribune.com/1985-12-31/news/8503300901_1_freedom-of-choice-coalition-margaret-sanger-center-first-health-care-center.

26. Kevin Osborne, "In his war against abortion, clinic fire bomber has no regrets," WCPO Cincinnati digital interview, 16:04, posted January 22, 2013, http://www.wcpo.com/news/local-news/in-his-war-against-abortion-clinic-fire-bomber-has-no-regrets.

27. "Order Granting Plaintiffs' Motion for Temporary Restraining Order in the United States District Court for the Southern Districts of Ohio Western Division," Gerhardstein & Branch Co. LPA website, http://www.gbfirm.com /litigation/index.php.

28. *Marian A. Spencer et al. v. J. Kenneth Blackwell et al.*, Case No. C-1-04-738, October 2004.

29. The attorneys for the defendant and the judge note in the court record that it has been a privilege to have Mrs. Spencer in the courtroom and they thanked her for participating in the case.

30. Alphonse Gerhardstein (plaintiff's attorney), case outcome described in conversation with author, April 6, 2014.

31. "Complaints against former NAACP officials dismissed," *Cincinnati Herald*, March 20, 2014, http://www.thecincinnatiherald.com/news/2014/mar/20 /complaints-against-former-naacp-officials-dismissed.

32. "Feisty Marian A. Spencer, 94, runs to catch a thief," *Cincinnati Herald*, December 13, 2014, 1; conversation with the author shortly after the incident.

BIBLIOGRAPHY

Books and Articles

Bell, Kurt R. "Tears, Trains and Triumphs: The Historical Legacy of African Americans and Pennsylvania's Railroads." *Milepost* (September 1998).

Blackburn, Judith A., and Robert M. Coughlin. *Building the Beloved Community: Maurice McCrackin's Life for Peace and Civil Rights.* Bloomington, IN: Trafford Publishing, 2006.

Blau, Judith R. *Finessing Segregation, Integration, and Independence: The Atlanta's YMCAs, 1858–1993.* New Haven, CT: Yale University Press, 1994.

Buchanan, Sandy. "History of Ohio Citizen Action's right-to-know campaigns." *Ohio Citizen Action.* February 1997. Last modified September 18, 2014. http://www.ohiocitizen.org/campaigns/rtk/righttoknow.html (accessed September 18, 2014).

Bundles, A'Lelia. *On Her Own Ground: The Life and Times of Madam C. J. Walker.* New York: Scribner, 2002.

Cross, John. "Whispering Pines: A Key to Success." Last modified April 25, 2011. http://www.bowdoindailysun.com/2011/04/whispering-pines-a-key-to-success/ (accessed August 14, 2014).

DuBois, Ellen Carol, *Woman Suffrage and Women's Rights.* New York: New York University Press, 1998.

"Edward A. Bouchet, Ph.D." *Negro History Bulletin* 31 (December 1968).

Evans, Henrietta C., John E. Lester, and Mary P. Wood. *Gallipolis, Ohio, Gallia County: A Pictorial History, 1790–1990.* Charleston, WV: Pictorial Histories Publishing Co., 1990.

Evans, Sara. *Personal Politics: The Roots of Women's Liberation in the Civil Rights Movement and the New Left.* New York: Knopf Doubleday Publishing Group, 2010.

Fairbanks, Robert B. *Making Better Citizens: Housing Reform and the Community Development Strategy in Cincinnati, 1890–1960.* Urbana-Champaign, IL: University of Illinois Press, 1988.

Feck, Luke. *Yesterday's Cincinnati*. Miami, FL: E. A. Publishing, 1975.

Foner, Eric. *Reconstruction: America's Unfinished Revolution, 1863–1877*. New York: Harper and Row, 1988.

Fox, Joan. "A Rarefied View from the East Side. Snobby? You betcha." *Cincinnati Magazine*, July 1985.

Frederickson, Mary E. *Looking South: Race, Gender, and the Transformation of Labor from Reconstruction to Globalization*. Gainesville, FL: University Press of Florida, 2011.

Friedman, Roslyn. "Marian Spencer Blazed a Trail for Justice." *Applause Magazine*, February–March 1997.

Grace, Kevin. *Legendary Locals of Cincinnati, Ohio*. Charleston, SC: Arcadia Publishing, 2011,

Griffin, William Wayne. *African Americans and the Color Line in Ohio, 1915–1930*. Columbus, OH: Ohio State University Press, 2005.

Huggins, Nathan. *Harlem Renaissance*. New York: Oxford University Press, 2007.

Hutchinson, George. *The Harlem Renaissance in Black and White*. Cambridge, MA: Harvard University Press, 1995.

Jacques, Charles J. *Cincinnati's Coney Island: America's Finest Amusement Park*. Jefferson, OH: Amusement Park Journal, 2002.

Katz, Robert. "Continuing Their Mission, Jewish Hospitals Reinvest in Philanthropy." Last modified June 18, 2008. http://www.forward.com/articles/13591/continuing-their-mission-jewish-hospitals-reinves-/ (accessed September 5, 2014).

Kenny, Daniel J. *Illustrated Cincinnati: A Pictorial Handbook of the Queen City*. Cincinnati, OH: Robert Clarke and Co., 1875.

Kessinger, Thomas A. "Legal Efforts Toward Desegregation of Education in Cincinnati." *American Educational History Journal* 32, no. 1 (Spring 2005).

Koff, Stephen. "A Hot Retort from the West. Defensive? You betcha." *Cincinnati Magazine*, July 1985.

Kornbluh, Andrea Tuttle. *Lighting the Way: The Woman's City Club of Cincinnati, 1915–1965*. Cincinnati, OH: Young and Klein, 1986.

Lewis, Tom. *Divided Highways: Building the Interstate Highways, Transforming American Life*. Ithaca, NY: Cornell University, 2013.

Loewen, James W. *Sundown Towns: A Hidden Dimension of American Racism*. New York: Touchstone, 2005.

Love, Spencie. *One Blood: The Death and Resurrection of Charles R. Drew*. Chapel Hill, NC: University of North Carolina Press, 1996.

McCarty, Mary, and Michael Graham. "Abortion: Cincinnati's Civil War: How will it End?" *Cincinnati Magazine*, April 1990.

McGrane, Reginald C. *The University of Cincinnati: A Success Story in Urban Higher Education*. New York: Harper and Row, 1963.

McWhirter, Cameron. *Red Summer: The Summer of 1919 and the Awakening of Black America*. New York: MacMillan, 2011.

Mickens, Ronald E. "Edward A. Bouchet: The First Black Ph.D." *Black Collegian* 8, no. 4 (March/April 1978).

Mijagkij, Nina. *Light in the Darkness: African Americans and the YMCA, 1852–1946*. Lexington, KY: University of Kentucky Press, 1994.

Moore, Gina Ruffin, *Cincinnati*. Charleston, SC: Arcadia Publishing, 2007,

Nolen, John. *New Towns for Old (1927): Achievements in Civic Improvement in Some American Small Towns and Neighborhoods*. Amherst, MA: University of Massachusetts Press, 2005.

Perry, Dick. *Vas You Ever In Zinzinnati? A Personal Portrait of Cincinnati*. New York: Weathervane Books, 1966.

Powell, Rachel E., *Lighting the Fire, Leading the Way: The Woman's City Club of Greater Cincinnati 1965–2015*. Cincinnati, OH: Woman's City Club of Greater Cincinnati, Inc., March 2015. Appendix I Timeline.

Quillen, Frank U. *The Color Line in Ohio: History of Race Prejudice in a Typical Northern State*. Ann Arbor, MI.: G. Wahr, 1913.

Rieselman, Deborah. "African American Heritage at UC." *UC Magazine*, last modified May 2000. http://www.magazine.uc.edu/issues/0500/legends.html (accessed September 18, 2014).

Robertson, Nancy Marie. *Christian Sisterhood, Race Relations, and the YWCA, 1906–1946*. Urbana-Champaign, IL: University of Illinois Press, 2007.

Rogers, Millard F., Jr. *John Nolen and Mariemont: Building a New Town in Ohio*. Baltimore, MD: Johns Hopkins University Press, 2001.

Rose, Melody. *Abortion: A Documentary and Reference Guide*. Santa Barbara, CA: ABC-CLIO, 2008.

Rowsome, Frank, Jr. *The Verse by the Side of the Road*. New York: E. P. Dutton and Co., 1965.

Silberstein, Iola Hessler. *Cincinnati, Then and Now*. Cincinnati, OH: Voters Service Education Fund of the League of Women Voters of the Cincinnati Area, 1982.

"Slave Narratives, A Folk History of Slavery in the United States," *The Federal Writer's Project 1936–1938, Ohio Narratives*, Vol. XII, 18–21. Washington, D.C.: Works Progress Administration, Library of Congress.

Smith, John Martin. *Angola and Steuben County in Vintage Postcards*. Mount Pleasant, SC: Arcadia Publishing, 2001.

Springer, Connie. "Don Spencer: 'What Cha Doin' Now,' To Make A Better World." Unpublished article, 2008.

Stradling, David. *Cincinnati: From River City to Highway Metropolis*. Mount Pleasant, SC: Arcadia Publishing, 2003.

Taft, Charles P. *City Management: The Cincinnati Experience*. New York: Farrar and Rinehart, 1933.

Taylor, Nikki. *America's First Black Socialist: The Radical Life of Peter H. Clark*. Lexington, KY: University Press of Kentucky, 2013.

Thornbrough, Emma Lou. *Indiana Blacks in the Twentieth Century*. Bloomington, IN: Indiana University Press, 2001.

Wilkerson, Isabel. *The Warmth of Other Suns: The Epic Story of America's Great Migration*. New York: Vintage Books, 2011.

Wolcott, Victoria W. *Race, Riots, and Roller Coasters: The Struggle Over Segregated Recreation in America*. Philadelphia: University of Pennsylvania Press, 2012.

Writers' Program of the Work Projects Administration in the State of Ohio. *Cincinnati: A Guide to the Queen City and Its Neighbors*. Cincinnati, OH: Wiesen-Hart Press, 1943.

Interviews

Brown, Yvonne. Conversation with Dot Christenson.

Gerhardstein, Alphonse. Conversation with Dot Christenson. Cincinnati, April 6, 2014.

Ginsberg, Enid. Conversation with Dot Christenson. Cincinnati, May 25, 2014.

Spencer, Donald A. Interview with Dot Christenson. Cincinnati, 2000.

Spencer, Marian. Interviews with Dot Christenson. Cincinnati, January–May 2012.

Wise, Henry Alexander, IV. Conversation with Dot Christenson. Cincinnati, October 27, 2005.

Online Sources

"African American History Month, 2002, Fox Lake: Angola, Indiana." National Register of Historic Places, last modified 2002. http://www.nps.gov/Nr/feature/afam/2002/foxlake.htm (accessed September 5, 2014).

"Cabell County History." Cabel County, West Virginia, last modified August 1, 2000. http://www.cabellcounty.org/History/history.htm (accessed August 14, 2014).

Coney Island. "History." http://www.coneyislandpark.com/history.php (accessed September 5, 2014).

"Dolls for Democracy," *Missouri Times*. Columbia, MO: The State Historical Society of Missouri, May 2009. http://shs.umsystem.edu.

"Guyandotte Civil War Days, Thunder in the Village," last modified 2009. http://www.guyandottecivilwardays.com/ (accessed August 14, 2014).

HOME. http://www.cincyfairhousing.com/.

Kenne, Steve. "Getaway Became Coney Island." Cincinnati.com. Last modified September 10, 2010. http://www.2.cincinnati.com/blogs/ourhistory/2010/09/20/getaway-became-coney-island/ (accessed September 5, 2014).

"Location and Population." City of Gallipolis, last modified 2012. http://www.cityofgallipolis.com/commissioners/population_and_location.php (accessed September 1, 2014).

"Marker #65-31 Gaines High School/Peter H. Clark." Remarkable Ohio: Marking Ohio's History. http://www.remarkableohio.org/HistoricalMarker.aspx?historicalMarkerId=1075 (accessed September 5, 2014).

Ohio History Central. http://www.ohiohistorycentral.org/w/Gallipolis_Ohio (accessed February 25, 2015).

"Order Granting Plaintiffs' Motion for Temporary Restraining Order in the United States District Court for the Southern Districts of Ohio Western Division." Gerhardstein & Branch Co. LPA website. http://www.gbfirm.com/litigation/index.php.

Osborne, Kevin. "In his war against abortion, clinic fire bomber has no regrets." WCPO Cincinnati digital interview, 16:04, posted January 22, 2013. http://www.wcpo.com/news/local-news/in-his-war-against-abortion-clinic-fire-bomber-has-no-regrets.

"Population for Ohio Cities 1900–2000," Cleveland State University. http://www.urban.csuohio.edu/nodis/historic/pop_place19002000.pdf.

Rastogi, Nina. "Who's the Heroine of *The Help*?" Last modified August 9, 2011. http://www.slate.com/blogs/browbeat/2011/08/09/the_help_kathryn_stockett_s_novel_gets_made_into_a_movie.html (accessed September 2, 2014).

Sonis, Larry. "Cabell County." e-WV: The West Virginia Encyclopedia, last modified May 31, 2013. http://www.wvencyclopedia.org/articles/792 (accessed August 14, 2014).

"State and County Quick Facts: Norwood (city), Ohio." United States Census Bureau. http://www.quickfacts.census.gov/qfd/states/39/3957386.html (accessed September 5, 2014).

"The History of the Negro Motorist Green Books." Lerner Publishing, Inc., last modified 2010. http://www.bpl.org/general/associates/history_green_book.pdf (accessed September 2, 2014).

"West Virginia Water Laws, Water Regulations, and Water Rights." West Virginia Department of Environmental Protection. http://www.dep.wv.gov/WWE/wateruse/Documents/WV_WaterLaws.pdf (accessed August 31, 2014).

Williams, Geoff. "Local Life and Lore in Cincinnati." HGTV. http://www.frontdoor.com/places/local-life-and-lore-in-cincinnati (accessed September 5, 2014).

Newspapers

"Black History Rich in Gallia County." *Gallipolis (OH) Daily Tribune*, Feb. 2, 1987.

Borgman, Jim. Editorial Cartoon. *Cincinnati Enquirer*, November 10, 1985.

"Community of Guyandotte full of rich history." *Herald Dispatch* (Huntington, WV), June 28, 2010. http://www.herald-dispatch.com/news/x1093607941/Community-of-Guyandotte-full-of-rich-history.

"Complaints against former NAACP officials dismissed." *Cincinnati Herald*, March 20, 2014. http://www.thecincinnatiherald.com/news/2014/mar/20/complaints-against-former-naacp-officials-dismissed/.

"Feisty Marian A. Spencer, 94, runs to catch a thief," *Cincinnati Herald*, December 13, 2014, 1.

"Dr. Donald A. Spencer In His Own Words: 'My life has been very full.'" *Cincinnati Herald*, May 8, 2010.

"Gallia County Emancipation Committee Nomination for 2014." *Gallia Hometown Herald* (Gallia County, OH), April 25, 2014. http://www.galliaherald.com/blog/2014/04/25/gallia-county-emancipation-committee-nomination-for-2014.

"Girl Twins Make Remarkable Record in Ohio School." *Pittsburgh Courier*, April 16, 1938.

". . . Here Warned on Segregation." *Cincinnati Post & Times Star*, January 19, 1972.

Kiesewetter, John. "Civil unrest woven into city's history." *Cincinnati Enquirer*, July 15, 2001. http://www.enquirer.com/editions/2001/07/15/tem_civil_unrest_woven.html.

"Local Desegregation Suit Is Postponed Indefinitely." *Cincinnati Enquirer*, November 6, 1979.

"Population Shifts Hamper Desegregation." *Cincinnati Post & Times Star*, June 19, 1971.

Sands, James. "Hunger for Education Common Among Early Blacks." *Gallipolis (OH) Sunday Times-Sentinel*, February 28, 1993.

———. "Stories of Success from Lincoln School Students." *Gallipolis (OH) Daily Tribune*, February 16, 1997.

"School Board Candidates Given OK To Discuss Desegregation Lawsuit." *Cincinnati Enquirer*, July 9, 1977.

"School Board Confident, Asks Trial Soon on Desegregation." *Cincinnati Enquirer*, April 19, 1978.

Shipp, E. R. "Cincinnati School Pact Is Embraced as a Model." *New York Times*, late edition, February 17, 1984.

"Spencer's Study of Communities Called Political." *Cincinnati Enquirer*, September 18, 1985.

"Study Shows Percentage of Blacks in Cincinnati Schools." *Cincinnati Post & Times Star*, July 11, 1972.

United Press International. "Two Abortion Clinic Fires in Cincinnati, Blazes 1½ Miles Apart Follow 'Mock Funeral.'" *Chicago Tribune*, December 31, 1985. http://www.articles.chicagotribune.com/1985-12-31/news/8503300901_1_freedom-of-choice-coalition-margaret-sanger-center-first-health-care-center.

White, Mary Linn. "I Hope I Never Feel There's Nothing to Do." *Cincinnati Post & Times Star*, November 21, 1972.

Miscellaneous Sources

Better Housing League of Greater Cincinnati. *80th Annual Report of the Better Housing League of Greater Cincinnati*. 1995. University of Cincinnati Archives.

Brown v. Board of Education of Topeka, 347 U.S. 483 (1954). http://www.law.cornell.edu/supremecourt/text/347/483.

Herz, Walter P. *America's Civil War: Legacies in Cincinnati, Facilitators Training Manual for Public Forum*. Cincinnati, OH: Cincinnati Museum Center, October 27, 2005.

The Links, Incorporated. *Links 60th Anniversary Report*. 2012.

Manual of the Public Schools of Gallipolis and Course of Studies & Regulations of the Washington Academy High School and Lincoln High School. Gallipolis, OH, September 1900.

Marian A. Spencer et al. v. J. Kenneth Blackwell et al., Case No. C-1-04-738, October 2004.

Republic National Convention, *Presidential Election, 1872. Proceedings of the National union Republican Convention held at Philadelphia, June 5 and 6, 1872 . . . Reported by Francis H. Smith, Official reporter*. Washington, D.C.: Gibson Brothers, 1872.

Wolf, Barbara. *Woman's City Club: Voices from 1965–2015*. Cincinnati, OH: Woman's City Club of Greater Cincinnati, March 2015.

———. "Woman's City Club Centennial." Video interview, November 11, 2013.

INDEX

Page numbers in italics refer to photographs on those pages.